Invisible Thread

10 things my mother never told me

PUBLISHED BY:
Assisi House Limited
The Net Loft,
Rosmellin, New Road, Newlyn, Cornwall TR18 5PZ
United Kingdom
www.assisi-house.com

Printed in the United Kingdom

First Edition: 2005

ISBN: 0-9548610-1-9

This book is dedicated to

my two daughters

Holly and Jenny

- thank you for the sparkle and joy

you bring to my life -

wherever your travels take you

may you always recognise the way home

and know that there is a

light burning brightly for you.

I hope you never lose your sense of wonder
promise me you'll give faith a chance
and when you get the chance
I hope you dance

(extract from Ronan Keatings' Single: I hope you dance)

INTRODUCTION

I have led an interesting, cross-cultural and infinitely varied life.
Rather like a kaleidoscope,
depending on what angle you are looking at it from, the perception could vary from bright to beautiful to some very dark corners,
to a heady cocktail of sensationalism.
I like Carole King's song 'my life has been a tapestry of rich and royal hue….'.it sort of recognises that in some way, all of our different experiences come together to produce a unique creation, which evolves daily, constructed by what we do,
who we are with,
and what we watch.
As the realisation of this dawns on me, I wonder what difference I can make to the end picture, now I know so much more than when I started.

After September the 11th 2001, people talked of eternity being 'only a breath away' and if that is so,
I wondered what I was doing that might last beyond my lifetime.
If I knew tomorrow was my last day on this earth,
what would I be doing today?

Despite being quite a shy person by nature, it is not unusual at parties to hear me entertaining people with a chapter from my journeys.
People fascinate me and over the years I have become experienced at studying individuals and groups:
what they mean when they say something;
what they mean yet do not say;
what they would like to say yet cannot articulate.
In over ten years of work as a Change Management Consultant and

Power Coach to senior executives I became perceptive and intuitive about human behaviour. Now as a single mother of two, I sometimes reflect on the high profile roles I undertook in the City of London, I recall the challenges of living in the middle of the desert with a Bedouin tribe and I look around my present landscape and find it every bit as fascinating, rich and varied, albeit a lot quieter.

When I completed my first book, *Thank God for Life*, I realised that in the light of eternity, much of my life could look like sand just running through fingers, not attaching itself to any particular framework. I also came to the conclusion that the happiest times were often when I had nothing, materially, yet I was being true to who I really was and what I was passionate about.

While selecting pieces of scripture from the Bible for Thank God for Life I began to understand what Christians refer to as 'the living word of God' for it seemed to me that each time I read a part of the Bible it related to me in different ways, dependant on what I was doing, how I was feeling, what I was thinking. This amazed me.

In my youth in Canada, I had dutifully trundled around after my mother every Sunday, to the Catholic Church I had been confirmed in, and I attended all the religious festivals I was meant to. I had no qualms about dressing up as a witch each year at Hallowe'en; it was part of our family and our community ritual. I don't recall anyone reading a Bible other than at Church on a Sunday.

I left home at an early age and stumbled through my teenage years and tripped into my 20's. How could it be that I was late into my 30's before I opened a Bible to really try and find some answers? By this time I was angry, frustrated and incredibly weary with trying to keep up a lifestyle that for the most part seemed very lonely. I wanted to know, if there was a God, just what he was up to, and why he couldn't make me happier.

At 40th birthday parties people wistfully lament the passing years and dream of what they would do if they could go back and do it again. I have no desire to go back and do it again; once was quite enough for me! Although if I could, I would wish to know more of what I know now - perhaps it would mean I would have achieved so much more of value; instead I reflect upon a shameful two decades of drifting and parties and scattered relationships until I was rescued by the birth of my daughter and finally woke up from my 'princess type dreaming' to what really matters - producing feelings of pain and relief all rolled into one.

Watching the documentary of the original creation of the Band Aid single, 'Do they know it's Christmas Time' I was shocked when the Artist of the single's cover, described the design process. I noticed for the first time the two Ethiopian children in the front of the colourful picture - I had never seen them before, despite buying the single when it first came out and owning it for twenty years. How could I have missed them? It took someone to point it out to me and once they had, it was obvious.

In my life's journey I have come to realise that truly, all that glitters is not gold. In the words of a comedian:

"This really rich chap on earth knows he's about to die and manages to get an audience with St Peter before it's all over.
He says, "Look, St Peter, I really want to come into heaven; however it's very hard indeed to leave all my money behind. How about I

convert it to gold bars and bring a couple with me?"
St Peter looks hard and long at the chap and says, "Okay, if it really is that important to you, you can bring a couple as a special concession - just let them know at the gate I said you could."
So the chap dies and arrives at the gates of heaven and knocks.
The gates swing wide open and the angels welcome him in, but say he has to leave behind the burden he's carrying on his back.
"No," the chap tells them. "Its okay. St Peter said I could bring it with me." and he explains that he has special dispensation.
The angels tell him they will just have to check it out and call St Peter.
"Hello, St Peter. We're on duty at the gates and a chap has just come up with a pack on his back and says you have said he can bring it in with him...yup...okay..."
They put down the phone and let the chap in.
As he is trundling past the pearly gates and moves up the road, looking around at his new surroundings, the two angels lean on the gate and look at each other and say,
"Why on earth would anyone want to bring paving stones with them?"

As I laughed, it came home to me that in the light of eternity, all the riches he had stored up to keep him cosy here on earth, ultimately amounted to nothing.

When I heard this I realised one thing I had known all my life was that the streets of heaven are meant to be paved with gold
and with that understanding,
creating heaven on earth seemed, in some simplistic way, to be linked with making money.
It took me a long time to figure out I had got that wrong.
So I got to thinking what are some of the things I wish my mother had told me, and here are ten of them which seem very relevant to the

world in which we live - perhaps something in them will motivate you to realise when you next see something and at a gut level know is a ridiculous sight, perhaps a ridiculous situation, you might just find the courage to deal with it differently.

It brought to mind the children's story of the Emperor's New Clothes and how the majority of people who surrounded him, just said what was expected of them and humoured someone who had power over them. Centuries ago in the Persian Empire, the Emperor, King of the Empire, referred to his wife as the Queen and I pondered on how she would have felt if she had been ordered to dress in the same invisible threads, how would she have kept her sanity! She couldn't refuse him as in ancient times men very definitely wore the trousers in the household so I thought about her moral courage in dealing with the situation.

I think she would have clothed herself with 'spiritual harmony' -
perhaps focussing on
love of her husband,
joy at the freedom of nakedness,
a sense of peace from knowing she was doing her duty,
patience with his latest phase,
kindness towards his gullibility,
generosity of sharing a tricky moment,
faithfulness to her marriage vows,
gentleness towards him for the inevitable revelation to come and
self-control when she would rather have abandoned him to his own foolishness and not embarrassed herself,
in all, retaining her integrity under pressure.

I know from experience that being clear about who you are and being able to live with yourself comes from a willingness to return to some of the innocence of youth, not an easy process. I figure the best that I can do, is to share some of what has happened to me and some of what I have learnt.

Telling the truth, living out the truth in all circumstances, you can survive - no, better; you can thrive on becoming all that is good and happy and honest and kind and creative.
- it's liberating
Go for it!

Carol Mote
Author

CHAPTERS

NEW LOOK • NEW FEATURES
antasies On Demand

CHAPTER ONE

Naked Men

I have always found it a challenge where to look when presented with a naked man. The eyes are instinctively drawn to his 'tackle', or there is the chest or arms; the face can be interesting - especially the expression watching you while you watch him......

Many a Monday morning, usually following particularly sociable weekends, I have made it to the gym to start Getting Fit. As days go, Mondays are a bit of a double-edged-sword to do this. It means you start the week with good intentions; however, it does mean you share the gym with the local rugby club who train there on a Monday. Wonderful 'eye candy' of course, however, as they press the weights and do all manner of things, you realise once again how far short your body will ever be from athletic prowess and if you are not going to reach that level, why are you bothering starting? As I thunder away on the treadmill I consider whether these fit chaps promote in me a sense of wanting to 'jump on them'............

It did once. I recall being at a nightclub with friends in my mid-20's and a very fit Australian athlete coming over to us offering us drinks and then sliding alongside me for a chat. He was cute. I had on a pretty short dress and just a pair of knickers underneath and before I knew it, he leaned over, pulled my cleavage towards him, had a good look and said 'you're fit'. I did what I always do when nervous, I just laughed. Several friends quickly advised that a slap across his face would have been a better response.
However the whole 'physical' thing between men and women to me

has always had a sensible animal level 'attraction and understanding thing' going on. I think men understand this better than women.

I have always had a dog; (you may be struggling here with the analogy but stick with me) and well behaved dogs have a very sensible social manner of sniffing each other's bottoms when they meet - not my cup of tea; however, I can understand they are just getting the facts straight.

So with this chap, in the nightclub, I understood he was just getting the facts straight. We had drinks, we had dinner, we went back to his place, he got his kit off, and at the point I should have been on cloud 9 with enthusiasm I realised I would prefer to go home. Not unsurprisingly I didn't see him again.

I grew up with this idea that for each girl there is a Knight in shining armour; that there was someone special searching for me, as keenly as I was searching for him, and when we meet we would know immediately, instinctively that we were made to be together forever. In preparation for this I can recall lying perfectly calmly in bed when I was young, hair neatly brushed, hands folded, my very own image of the Lady of Shallot, just in case he caught me unawares - I wanted him to be able to breathe in my serenity and beauty. Clearly, with hindsight, it would seem I was befuddled somewhere between a Disney movie and Fantasy land. My favourite bedtime story was 'The Glass Hill' a wonderful story of a Princess who on her 16th birthday is placed on a Glass Hill with a golden apple in her hand and her father says only the Prince who takes the golden apple from her hand, riding a fine steed, will be able to marry her. Eventually the poor woodcutter on his third valiant try up the hill, gets the girl.

As the years went by, the truth in life seemed to me that there was an array of men standing on their own glass hills proudly displaying their own manner of apples and like a demented hamster, I kept running up to get a piece, only to find after the first or second attempt, I couldn't be bothered with the third - not ever realising the self-perpetuating pattern I was creating for myself.

Wendy Cope wrote a great poem entitled 'Bloody Men' and it says:

Bloody men are like bloody buses.
You wait for about a year
And as soon as one approaches your stop
Two or three others appear.

You look at them flashing their indicators
Offering you a ride.
You're trying to read the destinations,
You haven't much time to decide.

If you make a mistake, there is no turning back.
Jump off, and you'll stand there and gaze
While the cars and taxis and lorries go by
And the minutes, the hours, the days.

which I thought summed things up pretty well.

There were chaps who wanted to marry me and I would think - that's it, I'll commit to him and it will all work out. The trouble is, when you are unsure of yourself, by yourself, you cannot sustain a permanent relationship with someone else.

Yet there was light (which you do need to keep you going). I met someone who was all the ingredients you could hope for in one package, although if I was considered to be living in the 'right part of town' he clearly lived in the 'wrong part of town'. We just couldn't make it work if he had to leave his tribe, and I was never going to be able to turn native in his world. As a naked human being, in every way, he remains one of the most beautiful I have ever seen.

And so years passed of drifting through relationships, each seeming so important at the time yet each sapping a small part of me.
Too much wine, too many hangovers and oceans and oceans of lonely nights, lonely mornings and days empty of real meaning.

A continual search for happiness and a growing sense that life was slipping by. I started to wonder when I was happy, did I know what happiness was? What was this elusive relationship thing I seemed to be missing out on?

As I looked at the picture 'La Belle Dame Sans Merci' I thought about vulnerability. In the picture, there is a beautiful woman leaning off her horse to kiss a Knight. At first glance you could say the Knight is vulnerable as he leans up to accept the kiss, yet as he has full armour on he is really completely protected. What a fraud, not vulnerable at all.

It made me consider that whilst a man might look vulnerable when he is physically naked in front of you, you can't see further than his physical form which is a purely animal based association. Is he truly naked at all? Are you? Surely it's not all just about animal attraction?

I went in search of a hero. I wanted a story of a real man who acted bravely and honourably to rescue and marry the woman he wanted. Having warmed to the Bible as an authority on relationships, it didn't take me long to search it and find the story of Boaz and Ruth. This to

me was a love story, demonstrating the power of pure love to overcome all difficulties. In reading it I realised that what seemed to be childish fantasies of honour and justice and love are not fantasies at all.
But I digress; let me fill you in on the story if it is new to you.

It was a time of famine and a chap and his wife emigrated to try to create a better life. In their newly adopted country they had two sons. Unfortunately in time the father died leaving his wife a single parent to bring up their children, which she did. The boys grew up and married local women, one of whom was Ruth. Then the sons also died and the mother decided to return to the country of her birth as she had heard that food supplies were now more regular, so she set out with her daughters-in-law to return home. As they approached the country border, she felt badly that the two women were coming with her as she did not know how they would be received back in her own village, so she encouraged them not to come, to go back and be with their own mothers.

This was a brave thing for the elderly lady (Naomi) to do, for arriving back in her old country without a husband to look after her, she would be very vulnerable indeed. One of the daughters-in-law turned back; however, Ruth insisted on staying with Naomi assuring her that whilst they might have a tough time, they would tough it out together. This was an honourable and spirited approach to take.

When they arrived back in the original country they were the talk of the town and Naomi was deeply grieved that they were penniless and homeless, having just a strip of land that her husband had left her. They found temporary shelter and as it was the beginning of the harvest, Ruth went looking to see what scraps she could get from the fields where the harvesters had been.

Boaz was a man who had distinguished himself in war and though absent when the two women first came back, on his return while viewing his Estate, he saw Ruth and asked who she was. Whilst he investigated their situation, Boaz, unbeknown to Ruth, asked the harvesters to ensure that they left grains that Ruth might pick up enough for both her and Naomi to be comfortable. Boaz then told Ruth to pick only in his fields and that his workers would not molest her or harm her in any way. What Ruth did not know yet was that through marriage she was related to Boaz.

Boaz was really impressed with the way Ruth behaved towards Naomi and towards others with her faithfulness, honesty, trustworthiness. When Naomi realised that Ruth was in Boaz's fields, she also realised the legal opportunity that, bar one other relative, Boaz would be able to marry Ruth, and so she started to act as a Matchmaker. Luckily Boaz realised the same thing and was also working on the situation; he met with the other relative and asked him if he wanted to buy the strip of land Naomi was selling and the other relative did not. Therefore in front of everyone Boaz bought the land and with it, the entitlement to marry Ruth. Boaz married Ruth and they had a son, and with Naomi lived happily - what a celebration!

Overall I think what inspires me about this story is the way in which Ruth left all that she knew to follow what was an honourable course. She had no idea where it would lead. In the East at that time the position of an unmarried woman was a dangerous one - only within the house of a husband could she be assured of respect and protection. So she moved from where she was known and her credentials established, to a completely new and foreign land because of the love and commitment to another human being (Naomi). Faithfulness is ultimately rewarded.

Although the women did work together to ensure a successful result, it was Boaz acting on his own initiative which impressed me most. When he first saw Ruth, he quickly assimilated all the facts of the situation and understood the dangers she faced picking in the fields yet he did not strike out boldly and brashly giving commands and ultimatums, he worked in the background to ensure she was looked after; not something she would ever know about - she would just have thought she was 'lucky'. Yet had Ruth 'caught' Boaz organising the food for her and Naomi, he would likely have been startled and caught in the headlight of her enquiry - would have stood naked before her as his soul was bared and vulnerable and I am sure Ruth would have been very pleased with what she saw.

In the 21st Century I think women sell themselves short. Women seem to have low expectations of men and low expectations of relationships in general. As I contemplate this in the light of my own experiences I realise, it's corny but true, that my low expectations came from low expectations of my father.

A father is a role model. In the 1960's when I was born in Canada, my father travelled a lot. He was a very gallant charismatic person who lit up a room when he entered it. He also seemed very exotic as he travelled all around the world at a time when such a thing was both extremely expensive and rare. Yet he never came to school events or sat with me to do my homework - he was never there for me as a person. After he divorced my mother we saw little of him and I do not recall a single conversation we ever had. If he was my role model for men, no wonder I expected so little.

Having now discovered however that my Eternal Father has been keeping an eye on me 'behind the scenes of my life' my perspective changes significantly. Within the light of eternity, I can be compassionate to the man who was my Dad (he died many years ago) with all the challenges he must have faced, and be excited about the amazingly gracious, honourable and loving Father who truly looks after me, over and above the confines of what we know here on earth.

Following that logic a bit further means I have a better role model to follow. Despite having kissed one too many frogs, and realising that I didn't need to have done that (patience and trust would have sufficed) I can start again. Had I stopped trying to make every man I went out with into Mr Right, had I stopped rushing into relationships driven by a fear of being alone, I would have lived a less stressful life and retained far more respect for myself.

I had a tough upbringing and it wasn't until my late 30's that I began to understand that. In a way I kept thinking if I just kept moving, if I just kept busy, I wouldn't have to answer the question about who I really was. I could also see by then that if I didn't deal with it soon, I would miss the best of the rest of my life - and I didn't want to do that. I wanted to live the rest of my life fully, truly being who I really was, and to do that, I had to find it out and I had to change behaviour I had had for years - quite a challenging but liberating experience!

Each morning the opportunity to become a more loyal and faithful person is open to each of us. It is quite easy in today's world to blur the truth of a situation, to 'switch the labels' to make something more bearable or acceptable. What an exciting day it is when we decide to start rediscovering ourselves and our dreams, when we awake to who we were, before we adjusted our thinking to fit in more comfortably with the status quo in society. What a revolution we start within ourselves, the day we rediscover the power of the word honour, and choose to live by it.

THREE THINGS I HAVE LEARNT

- It is not childish fantasy to wait for the right relationship, within the commitment of a marriage, before becoming physically involved.
- You can't hide from yourself, so enjoy the process of finding out who you really are and the dreams you have for your future.
- Our character is formed by the way that we behave.

My Mother never told me:

Pearl of Truth 1:

A man is more truly naked when his actions are revealed, than when he has his kit off.

CHAPTER TWO

Jiminy Cricket!

A few months after the birth of my first daughter, an old friend came to stay for the weekend to help. I was a single parent and to have a resident babysitter for the weekend was a thrill. In the process of getting reacquainted and his getting to know my daughter we remembered how much we had in common and decided to cross the bridge from 'just friends' to becoming a couple. It was a long distance relationship which proved to be a strain in terms of travelling for all three of us. I remember driving home from a meeting one day and talking to him on my mobile phone feeling very frustrated with the whole situation.

Unfortunately I have had a tendency all my adult life when faced with an awkward situation, to take a quick decision to try to solve every problem with a sweeping gesture, without thimking through the consequences.

That feeling came upon me in the telephone conversation and I blurted out a proposal of marriage to him, which as soon as I had said it I felt I should have bitten my tongue. I didn't want to propose to him; I might want him to propose to me, but what I really wanted was an end to all the coming and going, the packing and unpacking of bags. It was all very whirlwind, as quick decisions often are. All the wedding activity kept my mind off fretting about the relationship and onto plans for a great party.

In my mind a little voice kept questioning my motives; however, I refused to listen to it. One of the hardest compromises to me was the wedding location. I had always wanted to be married in Church.

I didn't attend Church regularly and he did not attend Church at all, yet I had a deep rooted wish to be married in the Church, which I squashed in order to be accommodating and not cause any ruffles.
We got married in a registry office, had a reception locally in the South, a mad dash up the motorway for an evening reception in the North, and in the bustle of it all I felt elated 'I was married' and tearful 'it hadn't been like I expected'.
We moved to the North to accommodate his job requirements and right across the road from our house was a Church. In all the time I lived there, it seemed to call to me, yet I never once went into it.

The marriage lasted less than a year and it took another two years for the pain to start to subside. In my initial haste, I had overlooked the number of people who became caught up in such an immense commitment, and therefore underestimated the shock waves and 'fall out' which reverberated for a long time after the relationship was over.

Over a decade later, I can look back and be aware of a persistent little voice inside probing me to question the way I was behaving, which I hadn't wanted to listen to. What a lot of emotional distress I could have saved us all from if I had just slowed down and taken time to really explore how honest my motives were.

In my studies recently I have been reading a fascinating book about a young virgin orphan girl who was beautiful, with a great figure.
At a young and tender age, she was taken from the town she lived in by her Uncle, who entered her into a national beauty competition.
She got past the first hurdle of being selected and through to the next stage of preparation. This stage meant a year away in a royal palace to be massaged daily with exotic oils. The process culminated in an audience with the King who would spend one night with her.

Following the night together she would then live in the Harem as one of his concubines and if he liked her a lot, he might call for her from time to time.

When Esther (her name) was presented to the King, he decided he liked her so much, after just one night, that he would make her his Queen.
This book, the Book of Esther in the Bible, has quite a lot for your mind to get around.
In order to be presented to the King, Esther spent months in preparation;
a whole year was spent just covering and massaging her skin with oil, all for the moment that she would be presented to the King who might, or might not, take a liking to her.
Imagine each day for twelve months,
waking to spend the whole day having oils massaged into you.
I know there are some women who would, indeed do, enjoy being pampered however perhaps even for them, this would be an extreme.
Personally, I would have found it incredibly dull, and an infringement of liberty.
Yet Esther accepted her place without arguments, the options for an orphan not hugely appealing: life without a family network, a low level marriage perhaps and potential poverty,
or Queen of the Persian Empire, hmmm?

And so they got married.
WOW feasting, celebrations - we can only speculate as very little is mentioned about the pomp and ceremony that might have taken place.
However, the crux of the story is not that Esther becomes Queen.
The crux of the story is not the public success.
The crux of the story happens when Esther is faced with a very uncomfortable situation;

after all she has been through,
she is Queen.
She has a privileged life
yet unknown to the King when he married her, she is a Jew
and her people, the Jewish race, needed her to intervene
by taking the risk of acting on their behalf, to save lives.
She could potentially lose everything.
Mordecai, her Jewish Uncle and closest Advisor, says to Esther,
"Who knows? Perhaps this is the moment you have been made for."
She was faced with being in the position of Captain at the helm
with her 'team' behind her.
She was in the right place, at the right time,
with the knowledge and an ability to make a difference.
A tough call.
A potentially very costly call.

I watched the rugby World Cup final. I am not a sports person myself.
I do not know the rules and I am not a natural spectator.
However, I have spent my life working in a job which involves helping people to move from one situation to another
and so I amazed myself that I found it fascinating to watch team play in action in such a vivid way, with so much at stake.
As the player gained the ball he had to decide quickly whether he could run for it or if the way was unclear, whom to pass it to.
The rules stipulating that they need to pass back in order to go forward,
the whole team needed to be mobilised, attentive,
fighting to become available,
seeking to be of help - as one moves forward, the whole team moves forward
keeping alert to what was happening around.

As the game ended, after the winning kick was taken
the player's mother was asked how she felt
'Well, I am not surprised,' she said. 'He has practised a million kicks in the garden - '
He was in the right place,
years of preparation behind him
a team willing him on
an urgency to act
and a world watching.
I am sure there was no Jiminy Cricket on his shoulder debating with him, whether he should kick or not. Some calls to action are very clear indeed.

By the World Cup Final it was clear one of two teams was going to win; in life, however, it isn't always clear who is on the winning side.
Many teams in life spend long periods of time debating their purpose and direction and even what it is they are meant to do.
Endless spiralling circles of debate
inter-bickering
without focus
or direction
or leadership.

As teams are made up of individual people with individual challenges, I started to wonder who was in my 'team'; my family, friends, people at work, those in my community, those in my home and at my Church. I thought of all these people and wondered, if they were lined up in the playground, who I would pick for my closest team.
I wondered if they would pick me.
I wondered if I would be perceived as someone who added positive

qualities to a team, with the ability for leadership; would I be a good ambassador for them?
Would others think I could react well under pressure, taking a tough decision to the benefit of all if required?

If had to answer to a team of people I respected in life, to a group I wanted to help grow more successful in a spiritual sense, I would have to admit that I let them down recently. Since arriving in Cornwall I had found it impossible to find work. Despite my applying for hundreds of jobs and attending several interviews no-one wanted to employ me. It seemed the skillset that had served me so well in the City was redundant in the country.

As I was walking my dog one day a friend rushed up to me and gave me a job advertisement which had been in the local paper. I read it and dismissed the role as one which would have an incredible amount of politics which I knew I was not very good at handling. Within two days two other people gave me the same job advertisement and suggested I apply. Whilst I had grave misgivings I thought there was no harm in applying for the role; at the very least I could tell the company my own thoughts on how they could improve their productivity.

No one was more surprised than I when I was invited for interview and I thoroughly enjoyed preparing my presentation on how I felt the role could be effective. The interview must have gone very well for then I was offered the job and at this point I stepped back and truly considered whether I should take it. Don't get me wrong, I needed the income. For the past six months I had been running a small painting and decorating business and whilst years before I could never have envisaged doing such work, I was beginning to build up a steady amount of business. In addition, I had a couple of cleaning jobs which I had just started and the two roles fitted in well with family commitments I had.

When I raised my concerns, friends and family pointed out that the new job was far more in keeping with my experience and provided a steady income. The role was dependant upon having a car as it involved considerable travel across the county. Some money was provided towards the cost of a car by a friend and then another friend offered to lend me the rest of the money to purchase a car.

Unusually for me, I decided not to rush into a decision and sent the company a carefully worded email, which I thought subtly gave me a further week to consider whether to accept or not. Unfortunately there was a fault with my computer and whilst I thought the email had not gone, and so re-sent it six times before rebooting the system, in actual fact it did go each time and so the company received seven emails from me which they took to be great enthusiasm on my part. In the light of my apparent extreme positive attitude to the role, their response was to add another couple of conditions to the employment contract.

I was now faced with nagging doubts on several fronts:
the new conditions to the contract,
the added debt I had incurred by getting the car and the continual feeling that it really wasn't the job for me.
Yet I did not have the courage, in the face of my friends and family supporting me, to be true to my heart and my reservations.
Despite misgivings,
I took the job and tried really hard to make it work.
Within eight months I had to face the fact that whilst I was caught up

in a role which was unsuitable for me, I was unable to fulfil what I really should be doing with my life.

When I resigned I became incredibly unpopular with a lot of people, not least the company who had to readvertise the position and try to find, again, the person who really should be doing the role. It was a very isolating decision to take and because many people around me did not understand what I did, they were quite cross for it seemed to them that I had been very foolish. To me, when I looked in my heart I knew however hard it had been, I should not have taken the position in the first place. I had taken it for all the wrong reasons and I recognised that the wrong road is never right.

I Remember, I Remember

I remember, I remember
The house where I was born,
The little window where the sun
Came peeping in at morn;
He never brought too long a day
But, I often wish the night
Had borne my breath away.

I remember, I remember
The roses, red and white
The violets and the lily cups
Those flowers made of light!
The lilacs where the robin built
And where my brother set
The laburnum on his birthday -
The tree is living yet!

I remember, I remember
Where I was used to swing
And thought the air must rush as fresh
To swallows on the wing;
My spirit flew in feathers then
That is so heavy now
The summer pools could hardly cool
The fever on my brow.

I remember, I remember
The fir-trees dark and high
I used to think their slender tops
Were close against the sky;
It was a childish ignorance
But now 'tis little joy
To know I'm farther off from heaven
Than when I was a boy.

(Thomas Hood)

It's harder as you get older to adjust the way you react to things; we get conditioned by what has happened to us in life. That little 'jiminy cricket' voice, when neglected, becomes faint.

I am a regular watcher of the English TV 'Soap' programme 'Coronation Street' and was dismayed when one of the characters, Jason, gave his mother a birthday present, not clarifying that it was from a friend of hers, not from him. He happily accepted the glory, thanks and praise from his mother, not telling her that she should direct it to the true giver. His girlfriend looked on and as they left the pub said to him, "You could have told your Mum it wasn't from you," and in all innocence, with a twinkle in his eye, he said, "I didn't say it was from me, she just assumed that." Such behaviour is dishonest, yet prevalent in the world we live in. It is often much easier to put a more satisfactory 'spin' on truth, which means it becomes fuzzy and the implications to ourselves less vital.

When I came out of our local Post Office yesterday, a middle aged chap stopped me by the telephone box and asked if I could lend him 50p to make a call to his home in Denmark in order that they could transfer some money for him to live on. He sounded Danish, he smelt of beer and I had just seen the lady in front of me refuse him. I suggested that he called the operator and have the charges reversed. However, he told me that it was his Bank he needed to call and they wouldn't accept the charge. I paused for a moment and wondered how genuine he was; I live in a village which has a lot of visitors and so know most of the people who are inhabitants and I hadn't seen this person before. I thought how I would feel in a foreign land without enough money to call home and I gave him some money, not 50p but £2.00 as I felt he would need that for a long distance call. He graciously thanked me and as I continued my journey home, he shouted out that he would give me £10.00 when his money arrived if he ever saw me again.
Back in the village later that afternoon, talking to one of the fishermen at the quay entrance, I saw the chap again, standing by the telephone boxes, smoking cigarettes, chatting with some people. I told my friend what had happened in the morning and he laughed and called me a fool. I caught the eye of the chap who had taken my coins and I didn't feel a fool; from his sheepish expression, I guess he didn't know I was a local either.
Never grow weary of doing what's right, even if it doesn't quite work out the way you expect.

In the book of Esther it records how her actions saved her people. Stepping back from the situation and reflecting on it, she realised she could not live with herself if she let her people down. The truth of that led her to take courageous action that would make her commitments visible to all, fully aware that in taking that action, she might lose her life.

Commitment is a deeply evocative word; it is less popular in today's society than possibly ever before.

People go out of their way to avoid commitment.

It has connotations of duty, loyalty, reliability, integrity, honour, truth and relationship.

People who make and keep commitments often do not know where it will lead them,
or what it will ultimately cost
or the deep joy they will feel when it dawns on them
that it's going to be okay.

Life is not a game of solitaire and often that little inner voice of conscience in my life has meant I have become a better team player,
noticing those in need more
being willing to commit to others who need help.

As you step up to the mark in the game of life
and you hear a voice of caution
knowing the spotlight of truth is upon you
holding the ball
you pause
what are you going to do? Will you pass it or run with it?
Who are you going to invite to play, who do you want by your side?
Who do you want running over the touchline and celebrating with you?

Who knows, perhaps next time at a crunch decision time, we will
realise it is one of the moments we will have been made for
and instead of it scaring us
we will demonstrate courage
and be a worthy team ambassador.

THREE THINGS I HAVE LEARNT

- Don't manipulate, use or deceive people; they are worth more than that.
- Listen to your heart more than your head.
- You cannot help someone become 'a better person'; you can only help yourself become a better person. Others may choose to learn something from observing that process.

My Mother never told me:

Pearl of Truth 2:

Acting with courage and following your convictions, is a defining moment in your life.

The ability to find joy in the world of sorrow
and hope at the edge of despair
is women's witness to courage
and her gift of new life to all

Miriam Therese Winter
North American Medical Mission Sister

CHAPTER THREE

And Baby Makes 2...

The international figures regarding one-parent families reveal a disturbing trend. It is estimated in the United Kingdom alone that lone parent families cost over £10billion in state benefits, yet this group of people are among the poorest in their communities. Over 90% are women and over 80% are aged 25 or older, which puts the 'gymslip' mother stereotype into perspective. I delved further and found that in all the countries I looked at, lone-parenting is on the increase. In the United Kingdom there are around 2 million lone parents caring for over 3.5m children - this is a big sector of society.

When I worked in the City of London and earned a lot of money, a huge proportion of it went on managing a home environment in order that I could go to work each day to earn the money to pay for the home environment. My job required that I was at my desk by 9am; however, the reality was I needed to be there by 8am and I preferred to be there by 7:30am. It was unrealistic to try to leave the office much before 6:30pm and 7pm was still frowned on by some, so arrival home was around 8:30-9pm, with work in tow. It was harder if I had to travel overseas.

My two children have different fathers, neither of whom has ever maintained contact or assisted in their upbringing. I had no family support as both my grandparents and my own parents had died and the children's grandparents on the other side never wanted contact. Therefore with two children, with six years between them, the needs were very complex.

They went to different schools
Had different pickup times
And sometimes had the same pick up times
Two sets of performances to attend
Two sports days
Two sets of homework
Two sets of friends and parties
And television challenges.

When the older was two, we had bought a dog and he (the dog) also needed tender loving care and walking and visits to the Vets. So I had an army of people supporting our life, a 'main' nanny, with others who either came in early in the morning before the 'main' nanny or came in the evening, an ironing service, a cleaner, various holiday clubs, a childminder as a back-up position - and all so I could go to work to earn the money to pay them to enjoy my children.

Eventually it became untenable. I was permanently exhausted and crabby, I never seemed to have quite enough money to pay the bills, the credit cards were mounting up, and I overcompensated for my lack of time at home with impulse purchases to alleviate my guilty conscience. The children enjoyed the presents, but more than that, they wanted time with me. Then one day my younger daughter came running up to see me when I walked through the door from work, (she always waited until I came in before she would fall asleep), she wanted a cuddle from her mummy and in complete frustration from a delayed journey home, I just screeched at her, "Just give me a minute". The look on her horrified face made my heart cry. It was time for major changes.
I called a family pow-wow.

The three of us sat around our kitchen table and had an open and honest discussion about how things were going. I encouraged them to be frank and they took this to heart. What came out was a vast array of different challenges that they had been facing, without my really recognising it; essentially I could see they would prefer to have more of my time yet understood I had to work to keep us fed and clothed. I recognised that none of us was really happy with the way things were. The girls and I agreed that the most important thing was that we had more time together and although that would mean less money, somehow we would cope. We voted to move back to Cornwall where we still owned a house, although it was badly in need of renovation.

The company I was working for had been going through a merger process and the role open to me following the merger would have likely involved more international travel than I presently did. After lengthy discussions we negotiated and agreed a Consultant's contract to work remotely with one or two days a month in London, and I resigned from my permanent position. As we repacked our bags in our rental home in Surrey to return to our house in Cornwall, I received a communication from the company to advise me that they would not be proceeding with the Consultant's contract after all. Without any income from another source, yet still feeling it was the right thing to do for all of us, I drove back to Cornwall with no idea how I was going to make ends meet.

On both occasions when I found out I was pregnant, there was no decision for me to make about not having the baby. Many called me foolish and stubborn and naïve and they could well have all been right. The responsibility of having children has, I believe, helped me to keep working at being the best person that I can be. When my first child came into my life, her birth broke the spiral of self-indulgence that I

had been wallowing in. I was no longer the centre of my world.
I wanted more for my daughter than I had had, not in material things, but in relationships, in being able to talk through feelings and emotions and be able to get along with most people, to become the best that she, (now they) can be. My children have been the greatest blessings in my life.

Despite all the challenges bringing up children on my own has entailed, nothing prepared me for the beauty of seeing them blossom into individuals in their own right, nothing prepared me for the awesome sight of their face lighting up when they see you waiting for them in the playground, or when they have had a bad dream and the only place they want to be is cuddled up beside you, or on Christmas morning when they scream with excitement at the possibility that Father Christmas has been. Childhood is a precious time of innocence.

Single parenting is a very difficult job. You have to be so many things at the same time. In any one week my jobs may include:

mother, nurse, cook, cleaner, washing and ironing lady, counsellor, dog walker, vet, doctor, nurse, personal shopper, food shopper, friend, DIY expert (or not), driver, advice giver, hotelier, secretary, taxi driver, telephonist, gardener, accountant, interior designer, technology specialist, teacher, hygienist, photographer, school liaison officer, hairdresser, homework specialist (in all subjects), disciplinarian, negotiator, referee, guide (on any manner of things from television to nail varnish) movie critic, historian, cyclist, window cleaner, seamstress.

Yet as a single parent myself I had no idea there were so many people, women, facing the same kind of stressful decisions and questions:
how to make the money you receive week to week stretch
which child is the priority for shoes this month

101 meals to make with potatoes, cheese and milk
how to keep up with all the extra munchies in the holidays
how to balance what is due on catalogue payments with the telephone bill
will the dog get fleas before you can afford some more flea ointment
and WHAT ABOUT ME !

When I stopped bringing in a regular wage and we had to sell our car, I found:

- the joys of shopping in Lidls
- that Tesco's own brand tasted okay
- cadging a lift with a friend is fun, but you spend more money than you should in the shops
- you can buy decent clothes from Asda
- I can balance six bags from Iceland on my bicycle, but it gets a bit wobbly going up the hilly bits
- It's impossible to live on income support
- the Banks don't love you when you really need them
- you can eat reduced price food without being sick
- debt collectors call on Sundays
- frustration is a very frustrating game
- my dog walks incredibly slowly
- both of my children have a great sense of humour
- I am useless at making decent pastry
- roses can smell very exotic
- there are a lot of nettles around blackberry bushes, but it's worth the effort
- you can be richly happy whilst penniless.

In bleaker times amidst financial ruin, I despaired at how my children would grow up. I did not want them to struggle the way I struggled.

I wanted them to do things in the right order, to have someone to share all the happy and sad times with. I have never talked negatively to my children about their fathers and if they have asked questions I have tried to answer them as honestly as possible because it doesn't really matter what happened in the past, it is their future that concerns me.

I have found great comfort as an evolving Christian, in the concept that God my Father really is looking after me and my children in every situation, in the tough times every bit as much as the good. As I struggled with no income, as we lost all of our material possessions, including our home, I understood more the value of what we had as a family unit. Tough times are character forming. and it becomes an exciting way of life to look for the lesson you can learn from any given situation.

GOD KNOWS BEST

Our Father knows what's best for us,
So why should we complain -
We always want the sunshine,
But He knows there must be rain -
We love the sound of laughter
And the merriment of cheer,
But our hearts would lose their tenderness
If we never shed a tear ...
Our Father tests us often
With suffering and with sorrow,
He tests us, not to punish us,
But to help us meet TOMORROW...
For growing trees are strengthened
When they withstand the storm,
And the sharp cut of the chisel

Gives the marble grace and form...
God never hurts us needlessly,
And He never wastes our pain,
For every loss He sends to us
Is followed by rich gain...
And when we count the blessings
That God has so freely sent,
We will find no cause for murmuring
And no time to lament....
For Our Father loves His children,
And to Him all things are plain,
So He never sends us PLEASURE
When the SOUL's DEEP NEED IS PAIN...
So whenever we are troubled,
And when everything goes wrong,
It is just God working in us
To make OUR SPIRIT STRONG.

Helen Steiner Rice

I opened the Bible, thinking about children from single parent families and how they might fare in the world, and I came across the story of Jephthah (I will call him Jep). Jep's mother was a prostitute and his father was a married man with other children. Although in his early years Jep lived in his father's house, as soon as they were able his half-brothers chucked him out and told him to keep away from them. What a nasty vindictive thing to do.

I could really feel the pain of exclusion Jep must have felt; the odds had been stacked against him from the beginning. Although he had lived in the house and had probably suffered from feelings of inferiority, it was still his home.

Fortunately however he was a resourceful chap, for he decided to take to the highways and became a famous leader of a band of outlaws. Meanwhile back in his home town, trouble was brewing and with a local war about to break out everyone started searching for who to turn to, to rescue them. The locals pleaded with Jep's half-brothers to get him back and for him to be made their leader.
Sure enough, cheeky as it was, his half-brothers contacted him and insisted that he come back straight away and rescue them all. Jep thought on this for a while and could see they might well throw him out again once the battle was over so he negotiated a good deal for himself. It was agreed upon and he dutifully, successfully, went to battle on their behalf. What an unexpected chain of events - the outcast welcomed back as a hero.

The tragedy of the story of Jep is that in his upbringing he did not have a parent who taught him and helped him to understand the intrinsic nature of God's love for him. Jep lived at a time when morality and religious values were in decline. He loved God and surrounded by many false religions that demanded blood and human sacrifice to worship idols, he mistakenly thought that God required the same. In preparing for his battle, Jep inappropriately made a vow to God that if God delivered victory in battle to him, he would kill the first person or animal he met when he returned home.

Having lacked a loving home himself, when he married and had a daughter he took special care to ensure his home was a place of security and stability. How hopeless all must have felt when he returned from battle, a conquering hero, and the first person to run out and greet him was his only precious daughter. The fatal repercussions of Jep's actions were inflicted on the next generation.

In today's world I think of the millions of AIDS orphans, in many cases the fatal repercussions of one or more parent's loose morals being inflicted on an innocent next generation.

We live in a time of religious and moral decline, we live in a time where people are searching for spiritual truths and have, at the deepest level, lost their way. As parents today we have a responsibility to teach our children how to connect with their Creator, how to build a relationship in which He can guide them, long past the time of our own, temporary parental involvement. In order to do this, we need to be able to make that connection ourselves, to recognise and respect the supremacy of the living God.

It is a great comfort to know that God blesses all of His children, those from inside a marriage and those from outside a marriage, and He can raise up any child of His to become a truly remarkable person, often in unexpected ways.

The most famous child conceived out of wedlock was Jesus. When his father died, Jesus became the oldest child in a single parent family. Despite his mother's controversial pregnancy and his humble beginnings Jesus is the most talked about man in history and now, over 2,000 years later, he is still making a positive difference to people's lives.

Ultimately, after all the challenges presented to him here on earth, he was crowned not with thorns, but with glory and honour.

THREE THINGS I HAVE LEARNT

- Forgive and move on; harbouring grudges makes you bitter.
- Don't give up. There is always hope, for God loves you and wants the best for you. Delve into the Bible for inspiration.
- The most important thing you can give to your children, is your attention.

My Mother never told me:

Pearl of Truth 3:

As a parent you are there to love, guide and nurture your child to become a citizen who adds value to the world; don't underestimate the complexity and beauty of this privilege.

God can make you anything you want to be, but you have to put everything in his hands.

Mahalia Jackson
American Gospel singer

CHAPTER FOUR

Sex in the City

Working in the City is a heady cocktail of money, power and distracting influences. It is like an island where you can come alive in a way you might not at home. I usually commuted into the City, only once living within its web. As I got ready for work, dressing in expensive suits and shirts, I gained confidence in my own identity. I would walk for the train, picking up speed as I went, fully aware that the quicker I walked the greater the possibility of catching even an earlier train. As my pace increased, a sense of competitiveness surfaced; my pulse quickened yet I felt cooler, more assured. I would stand on the platform at the same place each day and catch the eye of the same people, often falling into a fitful sleep as the train propelled itself towards London. Arriving at Waterloo, I would weave in and out of fellow travellers and head straight for the underground to take the City train, the 'drain train' channelling people off directly into the heart of the financial centre of London. Come on that daily journey underground.

"If I am pushed just one more time by that person standing behind me reeking of garlic I will scream. I will scream, I will scream - no I will not scream. Instead I will calm myself in my mind and wait patiently for the next tube to arrive. Pleasant thoughts of last summer on the beach with the sun burning down and warming me fill my mind, briefly. It is of course a million miles away from this underground platform with water leaking down from above. This concerns me and I look up again just as a drop lands in my eye. How can I be waiting for an underground train and water is dripping on my head? It makes me wonder if it comes through two or three ceilings before it reaches me and how much muck must be dropping with the water, now in my eye. I feel indignant; no one notices.

The couple in front of me are looking into each other's eyes lovingly and I cynically wonder if they had a very big argument this morning and are now making up; I resist the temptation to interrogate them.

A wave of grumpiness threatens to overwhelm me. My mornings are spent surrounded by voiceless people. We are all aware of each other, the smells and detail of each other - with no space between us strangers, it is very personal. On the first part of my journey I scan everyone's reading material and see the range of headlines across the national papers; in the second stage of the journey I am close enough to read over people's shoulders whilst being sensitive to their glances, and now on the final stretch to the office, too close to open papers, I am left to study people or look for the occasional rat scurrying along the underground rails. Not for the first time, it strikes me that the rats have more freedom of movement in these underground tunnels than we do.

As I hear the tube approaching I brace myself for the crush. Within seconds of the doors opening I am pushed and shoved and propelled forward onto the train. There are no manners or courtesy, no one helps anyone else, it is the most uncivilised part of the day. The doors close and I find myself face to face with the man who had been standing behind me; he smiles slightly and a strong wave of garlic engulfs me. He looks startled as I open my mouth to scream and clamp it shut tightly before I can make a sound. I close my eyes and repeat to myself, I will not scream, I will not scream.

Mercifully after a few minutes the tube pulls into Bank Station, the doors open and commuters pour onto the platform. "Good morning." I follow the voice to the left and see a work colleague smiling at me. "Hi, you walking or climbing?" We maintain our pace as we head towards the exit with a choice of a travolator or stairs ahead of us. "Climbing, skiing in three weeks," he replies. I nod and smile in his direction as if this makes perfect sense to me.

In silent agreement we start to climb the stairs; the 80 steps in front of me are old adversaries. On a steep incline they are a good work-out, yet I struggle to find the appropriate enthusiasm. In addition if I have to demonstrate how unfit I am, I would rather do so without a witness.

Predictably our pace slackens as we pass the third set of steps. Our conversation is brief - it is hard to climb and talk. This is not an uncomfortable silence; we are surrounded by fellow travellers following the same protocol.

My colleague is tall, blond and lean, married with four children and three dogs. He sells complicated technology to banking environments. My role in the same company is more basic and administration based. We work at the heart of the financial centre of London, where salary potential is unlimited, or so I am told.

We both live outside London and commute in daily. There the similarities end. I imagine that his house is further out in the country and has no relation to my one bedroom rented apartment in a busy commuting town. This daily trek to London is a grind I dislike immensely. The sole motivation for suffering the train system is that the financial reward in the City still outstrips that obtainable in any rural location.

"You're a bit later today?" I query.
"One of the children turned the alarm off and I overslept. I am normally in by 7am," he replies as we approach the last set of steps. This is not surprising news to me; public transport although still busy is more reasonable before 7:30am.

"Apologies, I have to fly; early meeting to prepare for. See you later," and abruptly he is gone, racing up the stairs, utilising his long legs to take them in three or four at a time. I feel deflated, I didn't realise I was holding him up so much. Sheepishly I look left to right to see if anyone has noticed; if they have they are polite enough to avoid acknowledging me.

I am exhausted. Why did I agree to the stairs, when I always use the travolator? Of course I know the answer; it is part of my eternal quest to look better in other people' eyes, part of my long term plan to move into a role with more responsibility. I have dreams of frequent exotic holidays, a sports car and a deposit for a sumptuous penthouse flat, yet no funding to match the lifestyle I would like to be accustomed to."

And so you arrive at work, already challenged by the day. A stressful and often exhausting journey into the office starts your day off at a disadvantage, particularly as you know there is a repeat performance due, in reverse, in around ten hours' time. A report published recently stipulates that London commuters suffer more stress than fighter aircraft pilots.

The journey into the City is like a bridge between your life at home and where you earn your money. Once you are on the other side of the bridge, you can interpret your home life in any way you want to; it is very unlikely anyone will come over your bridge to your home life, so it is protected in its own anonymity.

By the time you have entered the office environment you have adopted your work 'mask'. As you arrive at your desk you become who you are in that environment.

You get through your work and then you want to unwind, and if that goes well, you want to play. You have spent the day in crowded stressed environments with others in the same position. Home seems a long way away. Unfortunately this mixture of emotions multiplied across the millions who work in the City, creates a pressure cooker of raw energy and exuberance that is just waiting to be unleashed, and after work, down at the wine bar it comes out. Often it doesn't even wait until evening. I knew many people who started drinking regularly at lunch time; by evening they had found someone particular to play with and would book a hotel room for a few hours before heading home.

In my early years in the City I was part of that scene, though I found after work activities had to wait until at least Thursday night or I couldn't make Friday morning. I shudder when I think about some of the appalling things we did full of champagne and high spirits. There was no balance. It was an extreme lifestyle; if you missed out on a key night the dynamics of the relationships around you in the office could have changed significantly. Rich powerful men vying for your attention, it was a heady aphrodisiac. I can, much to my embarrassment, remember a night on the Strand in London when I had fallen over and a Policeman came and stood in front of me advising my colleague that if he, or I, did not take control of the situation, we would be arrested for disorderly conduct. I thought that was very amusing.

Luckily my colleague took him seriously and thrust me, unceremoniously, into a taxi.

It seemed everyone was misbehaving. It seemed the cool thing to do and the cool place to be. Yet on reflection many years later, and somewhat the wiser, I realised that very few people who were involved in this decadent activity were happy. Everyone was chasing something more than they had at home. After a couple of years I had to leave London. You will be pleased to hear that I wasn't chased out of town, I just knew the wine bars, the clubs, the intense partying, the on-off relationships with people whom you never really got to know beyond the City limits, seemed hollow and shameful.

No one had ever told me about the internal damage which is attached to casual sex, how churned up inside it can make you feel, how shabby despite the bravado you demonstrate outwardly. All the publicity made it out to be the modern way to be cool. As I finally managed to get clear in later life, God created us all to love one another; however, His directive is that sex is contained within the commitment of marriage. In having sex with someone you are not married to, and perhaps have no intention of marrying, you are messing about with someone else's future (or present) husband. There's an interesting book called 'Changing Values' in which it says:

"God's purpose in creating men and women is to make possible the committed and intimate relationship we call marriage. Only within this context can the goodness of sex find its true place. Sex is good, but like every other good thing, it needs to find its right place in the larger scheme of things. When sex is commended without regard for the wider context of human life, it is in real ways dehumanised, and can work to dehumanise people and make them something less than they could be."

In the process of evolution and in the name of fashion, virginity and a belief in the commitment of marriage has been brushed aside as outdated. Another book worth a read is 'No Sex Please We're Single'. It addresses today's perceptions on sex in a refreshingly straightforward way:

"unless you have had sex, you're not a real man or woman. You are incomplete, uninitiated and in some ways immature. What complete rubbish! But this is the implication of current attitudes. Those who have not had sex are seen as not being fully adult. Our perverse generation has managed to turn the self-control of virginity into a symbol of ridicule. Being a virgin is not seen as a badge of honour, but as a mark of being undesirable.
'Sexually honest' sums up the attitude of those who are not prepared to lie with their bodies, not prepared to say with their bodies that they are committed to a person when they - or the other person - are not.
Those of us who have disciplined ourselves away from pre-marital sex should not be bitter about what we have missed out on, because those who have indulged know that sex without commitment equals pain.
The painful path has been trodden by so many; the flattery, alcohol, loneliness or desperation that first got them into bed."

Many years later as a mother, I came back to work in the City and I saw things very differently. I had children to go home to; the after work after hours dimension no longer had any attraction to me. I could see others sucked up in it, as I had been. The most I could do was caution them at their desks not to spend the night there, or to send them home to sober up on some occasions. In one instance I had to organise a taxi to take home a very drunk employee who had fallen into a stupor at her desk - she ended up with a written warning after extra days off work to get over mild alcohol poisoning. Watching from the outside it all seemed very sad.

People fell in and out of extra-marital relationships and it was painful to watch the fall outs, hurting so many people. The dynamics of how inter-relationships work in the City, are more obvious when you work in the same environment. It is harder to explain to someone at home, waiting for their partner to come back, concerned that they are living another life away from you. The City at night is like a big Club for those with money to spend and out looking for fun.

I can say from unfortunate experience that if you suspect that your partner is misbehaving, they may well be. I have been in that situation and he remonstrated again and again that I was imagining what was happening; it was several years later before I found out, by accident, I had been exactly right in what I had accused him of, what I felt to be true in my heart. I knew the City, I understood the temptations and I understood, first hand, how something innocent can end up entrapping you into a whole network of lies and deception. Without great care you can become the type of person you least wanted to be.

You may have heard about the two cities of Sodom and Gomorrah talked about in the Bible - they were very randy places to be. My goodness, no-one was safe! The cities were rife with people misbehaving and sex was top of the agenda, with everyone and anyone who was available. It got so bad and such an insult to humanity, that God decided the cities were to be destroyed - they were a terrible blot on the landscape and it was known for miles around about the terrible things that went on within the city walls.

God's Chief Executive Officer on earth, Abraham, challenged this decision, said that it wouldn't be fair to destroy the good people in the city, that they would get caught up in the destruction when they hadn't done anything wrong. God agreed that wouldn't be right so He told Abraham that if he could find a good person, or people, he could tell them to leave - however He reiterated that the City would be destroyed and Abraham should act quickly if he wanted to save good people.

In agreement with God, Abraham found Lot and his family, and the angels who were about to destroy the city told them to run and not to look back. Unfortunately as they were running for the hills, Lot's wife look back wistfully and as she did, she was turned into a pillar of salt and remained there, fixed looking back at what was, thereby missing out on what the future held.

When we left Surrey and moved to Cornwall, and things grew tough financially through lack of work, I looked back with a degree of wistfulness at the City. I looked back wistfully at the steady and significant financial income. Yet I knew that if I went back, I would be lost, lost to my children, lost to myself. The price of being 'owned by the City' was too high for me to pay. It doesn't mean to say it is the same thing for everyone. I found being in the City like being on an island with all its own rules and regulations, unrelated in so many ways to my life at home which as an adult, I had come to value highly.

When I was in the City I spoke quicker, walked quicker, snapped at people quicker. I expected things to be done in just the way I wanted them done, when I wanted them done. I was far less tolerant and less sympathetic. I had significant deadlines to achieve and was surrounded by people with equally tough jobs. I worked hard and played hard and the adrenalin this created, refuelled itself spontaneously with the next big challenge; by the time I had journeyed home, I felt deeply exhausted in every aspect of my being. Yet somehow the next day, the cycle restarted.

Peace, tolerance, forgiveness, understanding are rare commodities in the City. They are 'soft' commodities and unmeasureable in an environment directly feeding into the world economy in a very measurable way. 'Soft' areas are at the very heart of human nature and an environment which does not nurture these areas will create friction within the human spirit, resulting in loss of integrity, ethics and morality, often producing poor behaviour - reflective of a human being performing under stress.

This spirit frightens me
And shadows me
And lifts me up.
I want to embrace its eternity
Yet I shy from its greatness.
How gentle is the hand of grace
That reaches down to each person in billions
And recognises their individuality.

As a Christian working in the City I could see things differently. I could see the mission work required to bring harmony to dysfunctional teams, to help mend or build bridges between warring departments, to help ease the pain often accompanying mergers and acquisitions, to help the lonely, isolated, marginalized, or poor in spirit to be a beacon of hope in situations which seemed hopeless.

In my early years in the City I, along with friends, used to laugh at a chap who stood on the steps of the Bank of England in his business suit, reading the Bible aloud, calling to people to repent of their sins and turn back to the one and only true God. I thought he was mad. When I last saw him when I was in the City, I thought how loving he was to know the truth and to want to help others save themselves. Regardless of those who called him a fool, he pressed on calling out to people, sharing life saving information with anyone who was passing. When he gets to heaven's pearly gates, I can imagine them being flung open for him and him being overwhelmed with a rapturous welcome for a job well done.

His story reminds me of Amazing Grace, one of my favourite all time hymns. The song is written by someone who made his fortune by running slave ships. One day he met and came to know Jesus - a love that turned his world upside down. Out of his pain and fresh understanding comes words of compassion and beauty and hope.

Amazing grace (how sweet the sound)
That saved a wretch like me!
I once was lost, but now am found
Was blind, but now I see.

Through many dangers, toils and snares
I have already come,
God's grace has brought me safe thus far
And He will lead me home.

The Lord has promised good to me
His word my hope secures;
He will my shield and portion be
As long as life endures.

And, when this heart and flesh shall fail
And mortal life shall cease,
I shall possess within the veil
A life of joy and peace.

John Newton (1725-1807)

THREE THINGS I HAVE LEARNT

- The wrong process is not justified by the end result.
- Channelling money into a worthy charity resulting in even one life saved, is a lot more satisfying than buying champagne out of habit.
- Work is your job not your identity; striving to be who you are in the midst of where you are, is an ongoing but worthy objective.

My Mother never told me:

Pearl of Truth 4:

There are no positive benefits to casual sex;
cross your legs and retain your integrity.

We don't call it sin today, we call it self-expression.

Baroness Mary Stocks

English advocate of women's suffrage and the welfare state

CHAPTER FIVE

Faulty Towers

Many years of my working life were spent 'headhunting' technology specialists to work for competitor companies. It often surprises people to find out that I knew very little about how computers worked.
I attribute success at what I did to be linked to my comprehensive understanding of how businesses work and the value I placed on effective communication and common sense. In many situations when interviewing candidates, with a view to potentially selecting for client presentation, I had to evaluate their true ability to accomplish the role under discussion. When people talk about what interests them you can see past what they are talking about to what makes them tick, you can see where their passions lie and often get an insight into their hopes and plans for their future.

In recruitment, whilst intellect is often a quantified measurement, demonstrated through exam results and project achievement, emotional intelligence is the 'x' factor and not everybody has it.

I enjoy going to the Science Museum in London and one of the favourite places within it is the Launch Pad where you can fiddle with various instruments which give you a different perspective on some aspect of materials that exist around us.

Whether you are young or old, the building blocks are a fascinating experiment. How high can you build a tower?
As you start building it is fun. There is a sense of anticipation and excitement; however, as it goes on and gets higher you can start to feel

really mixed emotions: pride at the accomplishment, fear that someone is going to knock it down - in the face of others who want to have a go, do you keep building or protect how far you have got, or do you let it fall and try something else?
Inevitably you know unless you stand there for the rest of your life protecting it, it will fall down and you will have to start again. If you stand and protect what you have created your attention is turned inward upon your own 'space' and you have no more time to try other things.

Someone with a high level of emotional intelligence would enjoy building knowing all the while that they would have to choose to plateau at a height that would stand by itself, in order that they can try other things. In effect someone with a high level of emotional intelligence can enjoy the task without taking it to a level that is stressful.

We live in a stressful world full of towers that we are protecting: career, money, homes, lifestyle image, fantastic cars - they seem so important when we are chasing them and yet even when we have them, just over the horizon still seems so much more attractive.

Towers have never been very interesting places to live. Historically they were always practical, isolated places to send someone up to watch from - watch for trouble coming, or good news, or visitors (which might be either!). They had long staircases to get up them and once you were there, the only thing to do was to look out - perhaps a good thing to do for a short period of time but certainly not a long term interesting position.

The first BMW I had as a company car was a sort of 'tower' for me.
I had so wanted one, I changed jobs just because I was offered one as part of a better overall package - it was the BMW which swung it. It was white and shiny and when I drove it I felt I had somehow elevated myself in society. I drove too fast in my BMW; it was made to drive fast in, but not in England.
In no time I had a speeding ticket.
Within only a few weeks, it was broken into twice and the music and the music system stolen.
On a journey home from work one day a hub cap came off on the motorway and when I stepped out of the car the wheel looked black and very tacky.
The insurance sorted out most of the inconveniences, yet it started to be annoying that there was always something I needed to be doing for the car; I got quite resentful towards it. My dream car started requiring far more attention to maintain it than I wanted to give it.
I decided what I needed was a new BMW, a bigger BMW,
not the one that I had. That was really a bit too old now.
There followed a succession of BMW's each one more lovely than the last.
What was I really chasing?

Image.
I somehow felt the BMW made me more interesting, more sexy. I felt I looked more successful, even if inside I didn't feel it at all. In fact what I felt a lot of the time in my job was complete boredom and what I did to cover it up was to rush around a lot, preferably in my lovely car.
The car soothed the pain of a job that did not either stretch my brain or require very much concentration from me. It was a very well paid job, one which lots of people would have loved to have, but for me it took little effort to accomplish and I didn't know what else to do with myself.

I was also trying hard to try to find a point to life, a reason for getting up each morning and going to work.
If it wasn't about owning a lovely BMW, a decent house and having a good job - what was the point? For me, it had to be enough or I didn't have anything.
I wondered if anyone would notice if I wasn't around. I wanted to put myself in dangerous situations to see if I could survive them; it was a way of feeling a thrill, which confirmed that I was still alive.

Sadly it took me many more years of floundering before I discovered none of those things will mean anything if you haven't got a humanitarian purpose to your life. Had I had some emotional intelligence in those days I could have saved myself several years of drifting.
Pride does go just ahead of a fall. I speak with some experience when I say - get rid of it before it trips you up.

Where I got confused was in thinking that material things are what we should be dreaming about. I can see now I just bought the advertising, not realising that real purpose to life is not publicised on mainstream TV. Once I 'clicked into' seeing there is so much more to life than self indulgence, I suddenly got a far bigger picture of the world we live in and became really excited about my relevance, in my sphere of reference.

Daniel is a great man of God in the Bible. He was a prophet from David's royal family and was carried as a captive to Babylon when he was very young. Babylon was an enormously wealthy place; it had enviable fortress walls, iron gates and hanging gardens that were among the greatest artificial wonders of the world. In the shadows of its glorious architecture, the citizens of Babylon were behaving shamefully, creating and worshipping all kinds of gods, practising magical spells and divination and caught up in their drugged state of euphoria they neglected those less fortunate than themselves with social, financial and practical needs.

When I first read the Book of Daniel I was amazed at the fact that God's loyal and obedient servants are often blessed with worldly success. WOW - I thought they were all poor. I simply did not realise that many people who follow God have been elevated to positions of authority, power and finance to provide practical help and hope to others. Taken into the Royal Court, then surrounded by gluttony, decadence and still a captive, Daniel managed to live a very saintly life, so much so that he was trusted and rose to the highest position in the State. So known was he for his righteousness, the King asked him to interpret a dream which was haunting him. In fact his dreams had become a nightmare.

In his dream the King saw:

"a tree at the centre of the earth, and its height was great.
The tree grew great and strong, its top reached heaven
And it was visible all over the earth.
It was beautiful and everyone came to it.
Then someone from heaven came down and said:
Knock it down
Strip it
Scatter anyone sheltering there
And let the mind of an animal be given to it
And in no time nothing but basic roots were left."

I am sure Daniel had a bit of a panic on how to tell the King the dream was about his kingdom and his days were numbered. Daniel however, was one of those people blessed with a very high level of emotional intelligence. Admirably following the path of truth at such a tough time, Daniel told the King that the dream was about himself and what would happen to him and his kingdom, for having drifted so far from God. Within 12 months it came true as Daniel explained it would; the king lost everything - until the day ~~the day~~ he came to his senses and said:

"I honour the King of Heaven
for all His works are truth, and His ways are justice
and He is able to bring low those who walk with pride."

The king had to have everything stripped away before he could accept that there was a mightier King than he. Recognising that there is a King of the universe is quite a stretch from thinking your world revolves around you, that rather than being in control you are in fact in service.

In recognising that the King of the Universe created you, you then realise that He must therefore know everything about you and everything you need, and you begin to understand that He wants to communicate with you and have a relationship with you. In accepting these dynamics you move into a spiritual world where you are a Princess in your Father's kingdom. With privilege goes responsibility. What kind of Princess are you? Proud, stubborn, unforgiving, deceitful, ambitious, cold? Or loving, giving, humble, kind, caring, generous, gentle?

As a Princess, are you aloof in a high tower,
or in the main square contributing positively to the lives of others?

Are your dreams of helping and going out to give to others, or nightmares with scary shapes chasing you?
As a Princess are you approachable or distracted with your own wants?
What kind of Ambassador are you to your Father's kingdom?

And perhaps most importantly, why do you think you were created? What purpose do you think you are meant to be fulfilling with your life? In the book 'A Purpose Driven Life', Rick Warren talks about the various drivers people have in their life, the things that keep them going each day: resentment and anger, fear, materialism, approval. He points out that knowing your purpose simplifies your life as it defines what you do and what you don't do. Without a clear purpose you have no foundation on which you can base decisions, allocate your time and use your resources.

When people used to ask me how I coped with being so incredibly busy I used to laugh and sing the song 'I'm just a girl who can't say no' as if it was in some way a badge of honour. The fact was the second line of the song was more insightful 'I'm in a terrible fix'. I have always found it really hard to say no to people as, until recent times, I struggled hugely with a deep rooted desire to please people - at whatever the cost to myself. I found it really hard to say 'no' because I didn't want people to get cross with me, I didn't want them to be disappointed in me. Therefore I would take on almost anything people asked me do, just because I was so pleased they had asked me.
I needed to grow up emotionally.

Once I discovered the purpose for my life, it became imperative to say no to some things, because if I didn't, I wouldn't find the time to do what I felt I was meant to be doing - I would be far too busy doing things that were distracting me from my core function. I realised that I had been looking for approval in the wrong place. I had been looking at people around me, at a similar plateau to me, instead of looking up and seeking guidance from the one person who has a perspective over and above all that we can see.

It can still be hard to say no to things, particularly if they are things that I like doing and know I do well. However I have to be realistic about what I can achieve in the time allocated to me. I may now be doing less; arguably, however, what I am doing, I feel I am doing better.

Being 'in service' has, in today's society, negative connotations, yet the humility involved in service is good for the soul. I remember thinking many years ago when I had a particularly unsavoury job to do, that I would do it for God and not for me or my work colleagues. In doing it for God, I set about completing it in the best possible way, and my standards immediately became higher. If the King of the Universe was sitting next to you in the car would you speak the same way if someone cut in front of you on the motorway? Would you drive as fast, with such a precious passenger? If the King of the Universe was with you in your office, would you take the sellotape home, or make the personal calls you do?

It is a great discipline to think that God is watching everything you do. God is interested in the detail of your life and how you work, help and serve others. He is interested in your relationships and in the way you speak to people. Perhaps one of the keys to improving the world we live in is to become better servants to others. Rather than focusing on the height of our own towers, we could actively help others to start building, adapting our designs to create more supportive, inclusive communities.

There is a Royal Decree declaring that all those who serve others will go to the Ball. Be excited, be very excited. We have so much to be thankful for and a lifetime to share all we have with those in need.

THREE THINGS I HAVE LEARNT

- Suicide is not an option (voluntary or involuntary). When you realise you are cornered, you can't just jump out of the window, you have to walk back down and reconsider your design.
- Our God wants to bless us, richly. We have to trust Him however and put Him first in all areas.
- It is hard work and takes practice to become a Princess in your heart and even more effort to live out your life as a good Ambassador to your Father's Kingdom.

My Mother never told me:

Pearl of Truth 5:

You can change your situation for the better by figuring out who you really are and what you are meant to be doing with your life. It may be difficult and it may take a long time; however, it is worth striving for.

ASE

CHAPTER SIX

Retail Therapy

School life to me was for the most part a tortuous existence. My home was an unhappy place to be, particularly from when I started secondary school at the beginning of the 1970's. On one level, I looked forward to going to school to get away from home; on the other hand with no-one at school with whom I could really relate to, it was a very isolating place to be.

Although I attended a Catholic school, there were no teachers or Church representatives who paid any attention to me as an individual or who suspected the troubled home life which existed behind the façade of normality presented to the school. No one ever questioned whether there was a deeper reason for my rebellious behaviour, no one ever sat me down and asked me why I slipped from first in the top class for most things to scraping through exams.

The girls whom I hung around with had traditional family environments and found my own home life very odd indeed. I loved visiting one friend in particular as her parents represented just the kind of stability I had always craved; when I stayed overnight her father would even request that I leave my shoes outside with those of my friends, so he could clean them for me. Someone made me breakfast, and dinner, and we went out on happy family outings - each time I stayed there I felt calm and peaceful; it was like being on holiday, and visiting a foreign land.

Yet, inevitably I would return home. I knew the rules at home and I loved it for it contained all the people in the world who meant the most to me, yet it was often tricky territory to navigate.

We had left Canada for England when I was 10. At the same time that we departed on a plane bound for Manchester my father left Canada to start a new life with his mistress (later wife number 2) in Germany. We arrived in Manchester to be met by my mother who had left Canada six months previously. In our time apart we had changed. As oldest daughter I had assumed a lot of the 'motherly' roles linked to overseeing my siblings and she had spent six months trying to come to terms with the dramatic changes taking place in her life, in our lives. From the point of our reunion at the airport, for the next seven years, as my mother wrestled with the pain of the man she loved divorcing her, I wrestled with irresponsible adult behaviour and the loss of childhood.

School didn't realise that I couldn't be part of any team which met outside school hours - there was no-one to take me to team events. I couldn't stay on after school, I had to get home and cook dinner and do 101 other chores. School just thought I was a loner, standing off on one side. I guess more than anything, school didn't understand that if I did spend any time away from home, I would fret about my siblings back at home without me, and I would certainly pay the cost when I returned. The worst of home life was the long nights of verbal abuse from my mother. All the venom she held inside for the downward spiral she felt trapped in would be hurled out, directed at me, until she fell asleep and an uneasy peace would reign until the morning.

As a young woman I felt powerless in every area of my life. I knew I looked like a female version of my father, a similarity which irritated my mother on a daily basis. My father however was rarely around; we had occasional visits from him but a lot more days were spent ready to go, when he never turned up. In hindsight why would the poor chap want to visit? When he did my mother couldn't cope, and subsequently we found it very hard too. When he was with us my mother would carefully select her words, balancing between needing his financial goodwill and wanting to hit him. When we returned from occasional visits out with him, the limitless questions and probing were exhausting.

In the midst of the island of pain which we lived on, my mother would often screech at me, 'Who do you think you are? The Queen of Sheba?" and as my blood boiled deep inside, I used to think she was mad. A queen? Me? With power and elegance? Where was she getting these ideas from? (As attractive as it sounded.) The cool exterior I had adopted as a survival mechanism suddenly gained an exotic air to it and I nurtured it.

Eventually my mother went away to a recovery unit and with us abandoned by the rest of the family, including my father, I left school at 15 and started office- based administration and typing work. It was sheer joy to earn some money, utter bliss to have a wage to buy myself and two younger siblings food. There was no money coming from anywhere else yet the three of us had a period of relative calm and happiness.

For me it was an oasis. The money I earned didn't pay enough to cover all the bills; however, I concentrated it on food and clothing and we had sufficient. Our family unit lived in a Housing Association flat by then and I managed to negotiate a period of grace for some of the bills, for a few months, until my mother was due to return.

I enjoyed working. I liked the sense of righteousness of working and then receiving money for what I had done. That sounds basic I know, but it gave me a real sense of worth and an inkling of power. Friday nights became happy times of celebration when I would come home with food for the weekend and a special Friday treat. Finally I felt I had found a way to gain a level of control. Earning money, having a bit of money in my pocket, gave me a new sense of freedom.

The pattern of money in pocket, ability to shop, became a preferred way of dulling the pain of living for many years. If I was cross with someone, I might go and buy something for myself. If I split up with a boyfriend, I would go and spend money on myself. If I was in love, I would probably go and buy something for him. Why did I love spending money? Because I could, because I had the power to walk into a shop and decide what I wanted to buy and someone would wait on me.

Mostly when I could, until I had children, I spent money on me and those who were immediately around me. I found not only did I love spending money, I was really good at it! I could get through my salary faster than I could earn it and then I discovered you could even spend more than you earned and with a bit of financial juggling, still keep going. I had no idea what dangerous territory I was starting to wade into.

Then I began to feel a bit like the Queen of Sheba. Here I was spending money as I felt like it, with no eye on the future, lavishing gifts on those who pleased me, and rising above any nitty gritty considerations such as 'the treasury is empty'. Yet the funny thing was, not even all this spending was making me happier. The point of spending, at the till when I paid or signed my name, was a thrill. Later however, it was gone again, a bit like a 'hit' of a drug which needs to be continually refuelled. I recognised that, strangely, I had felt better about myself when I lived quite a basic life in the flat with my siblings, week by week managing on the money I brought home. Even the times when I earned huge sums of money and could, and did, spend lots of it, it still seemed so shallow.

So I decided to find out something about the Queen of Sheba.
What an amazing story! The land over which the Queen of Sheba ruled was one of the primary centres of commerce of its day. Her own palace was renowned for its opulence; she would have had access to all the best shops, finest jewels and skilled craftsmen. Every possible material need she had would have been quickly satisfied through the abundance of choice right there, where she lived. Yet it wasn't enough. All the worldly goods available to her were not enough to satisfy her. Then she heard about King Solomon who apparently could answer any questions.

So with all the worldly goods she could possibly want or need, she went shopping for something she couldn't find in her own, independent world - wisdom.
She packed up lavish and generous gifts and set off to quiz King Solomon about the meaning of life. When she got to his palace, she could not believe it was even more beautiful and splendid than her own. She thought she had the best, yet here she was in a neighbouring kingdom and it was exquisite. Undoubtedly what she discovered was that the overriding difference between the two kingdoms was the peace found in Solomon's, a sense of balance, a way of life where people were satisfied, knowing that they were serving a wise King. The Queen of Sheba recognised that Solomon served a far greater King and

complimented him on the evident happiness and prosperity of his way of life and of his leadership.

King Solomon listened to her and counselled her. She in turn questioned him thoroughly on every subject that was on her heart and he led her in the realisation that more important than anything material, was the wisdom to understand life, and our basic need to be in relationship to God. So assured by the truth of all that King Solomon had told her, she gave away all the goods she had with her, riches on a scale never seen before in that area.

Many years ago I undertook training to work as a volunteer on the Samaritans telephone network. I felt having been through some challenging times in my life, I might be of help to someone else who was struggling. The hardest part of the training was the directive to listen and not to give advice. To unconditionally listen to someone who is in deep pain and may repeat their problems again and again and again and not to offer any kind of solution forward, took remarkable self-discipline on my part. It is a gift to be a good listener. Most people don't really listen to each other at all; they hear what they want to hear, editing out the bits which they find boring or repetitive as someone is speaking. The surprising part of being a good listener is you find that the person talking often talks around and around an issue and, with gentle prompts, gradually moves closer, through their own insights, to finding the answers that are right for them.
If you tell people what to do, you are imposing your interpretations, based on your experience, into their issue and because they have not reached that conclusion through their own exploration, it is unlikely to become a lasting solution.

When King Solomon became King and God asked what he wanted, he asked for wisdom above all else. A key ingredient to his wisdom was being a good listener. It is interesting to see that as time passed and King Solomon ruled his kingdom with wisdom, worldly wealth came also, yet the heart and priority of his Kingship was service and faithfulness to God.

One of the greatest joys of becoming a Christian is the growing understanding of the interdependencies of human beings. That you can make a positive difference in the world. That the giving of money to charity can help another human being live another day, perhaps pain free. That regular giving of money, which a charity can then bank on, can fundamentally help change the life of a person, or village, perhaps paying for a teacher, the building of a well or a herd of goats to provide a livelihood.

When I now have an urge to 'do a bit of retail therapy' I question what is really going on in my heart. Am I covering up some deeper need or do I just want to splurge some money? If I find it's a deeper need, rather than heading for the shops I tend to head off to a friend's house to get someone else's insight and in talking it through, usually find the answers. If it's a deep desire to splurge some money I question whether I have it to 'blow', and if I do, I am now more likely to give it to charity instead. Over time, the impulse to splurge money dissipates. Cultivating an instinct to give away rather than to keep is not virtuous, it's quite selfish really. It feels better giving to people who have real and basic needs for survival, than buying yet another pair of shoes.

I knew someone once who had a bedroom cupboard with around twenty unopened boxes of shoes, beautiful shoes, and many many unused handbags. Her pleasure in life was spending money on herself and then squirreling her purchases away so that very few people knew about them. She was always quite an unhappy person, making snide remarks to her husband, parcelling the children off to childminders rather than looking after them, never working - and she had no intention of doing so. She would only wear designer labels and mix with people who lived in better houses than she did. Her husband was a lovely gentle man who worked hard in the City and yet I knew from her disclosures over the credit card bills, they were chained to debt that he never saw the full extent of. She never gave anything to anyone else because she said she didn't have any spare money. In a sense this of course was true. However in the same breath she would go out and buy another pair of shoes. Shopping was an addiction and nurturing that addiction was the only life she really knew - the only time she seemed to feel truly alive and passionate was when she was shopping. She was wonderful to be with in the shops: she was excited and inquisitive, insightful and encouraging. She knew the price of everything, the fashions and the styles, she knew quality from tat and had no interest in anything outside the world as she knew it.

What a rude awakening she would have on a day of reckoning, coming face to face with God who said
"Did you feed me when I was hungry?
Did you clothe me when I was naked?
Did you talk to me when I was lonely?
Did you give me shoes when my feet were bare?"
And I could imagine her blustering a bit and saying, "Well, where were you? I would have done it if I had seen it was you."
And God would look at her with compassion, helping her to remove the veil from her eyes. "All peoples of the world are my children, I was there on the street corner in your town, in the woman's refuge, in the hospice dying for someone to read to me, in Sudan, Rwanda, Iraq,

Burma. There are others who know where I am, charity organisations, Churches. Did you try and find me? Did you search for me?
You missed the point of living, for your attention and interests were in the wrong places. You never tried to change direction from the route to the shops."

If I was called the Queen of Sheba now, I think I would ask "which one?" The one who lived an aloof and privileged life before meeting King Solomon, or the one who was changed as a result of meeting the King and who, through that meeting, became more aware of humanity and the deep and basic need for us to love and practically support each other.

THREE THINGS I HAVE LEARNT

- If you don't face what happened to you in your youth, you will spend your adult life trying to hide from it.
- Balance the enjoyment of shopping for what you want, with giving lavishly to those in need.
- When in doubt, seek counsel from someone whose wisdom you respect.

My Mother never told me:

Pearl of Truth 6:

All the riches of this world amount to nothing without a healthy perspective on our eternal purpose.

If you judge people you have no time to love them

Mother Teresa

CHAPTER SEVEN

Friends

A really positive impact of having had a lot of jobs, moved many times and travelled considerably is that you end up knowing a lot of people. Also, you learn how to make friends in any situation.

Over 20 years ago, at the time of the war between Israel and Lebanon I decided to go and live in Israel to try to understand the conflict better. Much to the shock and horror of friends and family, I booked a one-way ticket and in no time at all was deposited on the runway at Ben Gurion airport in Tel Aviv with other passengers and our bags. As we watched, the plane we had arrived on immediately took off again. Due to the fact that we had just entered a war zone, no other flights were due for awhile.

Although we were in a country at war, it wasn't clear who were the good guys and who were the supposedly 'bad' guys. Despite this, or perhaps because of it, friendships were quickly made. There were a lot of freely available drugs and a cosmopolitan mixture of people from across the world, all looking for something or running from someone. Passions often ran high over quite inconsequential things. Each day seemed to last forever. 21 year old Israeli Tank Commanders wandered around talking to foreigners to try to talk out their battle experiences, warily avoiding the numerous amount of American Vietnam veterans who were running from their own demons.

I quickly formed a friendship with another girl and we travelled together, sharing a room in the various Kibbutz we worked at.

We looked quite an odd couple, she with long blonde hair and I with long dark hair. I looked quite Israeli and quickly picked up some Hebrew resulting in my fitting into the background in most places we went. However she was a different matter. Her blonde hair was very attractive to many and we were often warned of the dangers of travelling without the protection of a bigger group.

Our intense friendship, formed due to mutual need, ended when she met and fell in love with an English chap who was also travelling; eventually they went their way and I faced the reality that even seemingly deep friendships can prove to be very transitory.

A new English girl arrived at the place I was staying, whilst I was at work. When I got back the group of people I tended to spend time with rushed up to tell me excitedly that this girl had arrived and was a model. They thought she was just the best thing to have arrived in days. When I met her, interested to hear more, I found her to be quite cagey about details and as she made sweeping generalisations about where she came from and I knew first the county, then the town, then the village and then the street she became frustrated that the identity she had decided upon for herself started to slip away. Faced with her discomfort, I stopped questioning her. Ours however was always a tentative friendship for I was never sure of her sincerity.

'Best Friends' seem to come and go. When I was 10 it was a girl in my class and the pair of us were always getting into tricky situations and mad escapades. When I was 14 it was a girl whose father was in the army. She got me into a different kind of trouble altogether. She was 16 and on very good terms with quite a few of the troops. In no time I was writing to a soldier which quickly escalated to him turning up one day on my doorstep (believing me to be much older than I was). My friend had suggested that I wrote CHIP (Come Home I'm Pregnant) on the back of the envelope on a letter to him; as I had not met the chap, I had no idea that he would react so strongly! I was made to apologise to the soldier, and my friend and I were banned from seeing each other for a while after that episode. Still we managed to creep out and meet up. As I look back I can see we all attract different kinds of people to be our friends, and there are patterns.

A favourite book during my teenage years was 'How to win Friends and Influence People' by Dale Carnegie. What a brilliant read! It is full of common sense and great fun to practise. In it, one of the many gems he reveals is "a hundred years before Christ was born, a famous old Roman poet, Publilius Syrus remarked We are interested in others, when they are interested in us."

I used to think that there are friends for different things. Friends you like to go drinking with, others you prefer to shop with, some perhaps you don't see very often and others you see or talk to practically every day. With good friends you haven't seen for ages, you seem able to pick up your last conversation where you left off, and with best friends you can know each other so well you seem to anticipate when they need you.

I looked up in the dictionary what it said about friends and it said a friend was 'someone joined to another in intimacy and mutual benevolence apart from sexual or family love.' The secondary explanation was 'someone you are on good terms with.' What a world of difference between the two statements.

I wondered then what words Roget's Thesaurus would associate with 'friend' and the only one it had was 'confidant' although it went on to say that a best friend was 'an alter ego' (which I thought interesting). Aristotle spoke of friendship as 'a single soul dwelling in two bodies' and Frank Crane said a friend was someone 'with whom you dare to be yourself.'

In his book on Friendships, Ralph Waldo Emerson wrote:

> I do not wish to treat friendships
> daintily, but with roughest courage.
> When they are real, they are not glass
> threads or frostwork, but the solidest
> thing we know. The sweet sincerity
> of joy and peace, which I draw from
> this alliance with my sister's soul,
> is the nut itself, whereof all nature
> and all thought is but the husk and shell.

Most friendships however seem to operate on a mutually agreed basis of behaviour. Once the agreements have been set up, if the behaviour of either friend changes dramatically for any reason, the friendship could hit the rocks. Friendships that are formed at very painful times in our life will either last for a very long time or vanish completely when the crisis, perhaps a 'shared crisis', is over. As I pondered on it, it seemed to me that most friendships have some level of 'small print' to them which surfaces from time to time.

In my teenage years through to my thirties I had a very deep friendship with a girl I met with a crowd in the local wine bar one rowdy Friday night. On some levels we grew up together. I went to her wedding, moved next door to her, our oldest children were born at similar times. It was a very close relationship; we trusted each other with our deep buried hurts and dreams for the future. Then as my career started to excel, her home life faced some real challenges. I tried to help; however, in a relatively short space of time our worlds had become poles apart. One day after a really painful and difficult issue between us, she stopped talking to me and never spoke to me again. It took me a long time to accept that the many years we had known each other and cried and laughed together and shared so much together were over forever. Small print, that I hadn't even been aware of, had appeared and I had to accept that not to last a storm, it wasn't really a friendship at all.

The greatest friendship I ever read about was David and Jonathan in the Bible. David had been a shepherd boy who killed a giant called Goliath. He was also an accomplished musician and was brought to Court to play for the King, who welcomed him into his own family. Jonathan was the King's son and he and David became firm friends growing up together in the court. They grew to love each other as brothers worshipping the same God. In time as David's success as a military leader started to overshadow the King's own success, the King grew jealous of David and kept putting him in difficult situations hoping he would fail. In the end the King tried to kill David and David fled for his life. Jonathan and David met up and assured each other of their eternal friendship and love, yet well aware they were unlikely to share more laughter until they met again, on the other side of death. Jonathan died in battle and the King was badly wounded and called to one of his own soldiers to end his life and he died next to his son.

When David heard of Jonathan's death, and that of the King, he and his army mourned and wept and fasted. David was deeply grieved by Jonathan's death and said, "I am distressed for you, my brother Jonathan; greatly beloved you were to me."

The strength of their friendship lasted through many testing years and outside influences. Yet in all the changing circumstances, they remained true and honourable both to each other and to others they were in relationship with, including their wives, their family, other friends and work mates. In studying the scripture you can see that the binding of their friendship was their faith - both believed in one true and eternal God and both served their God as their primary focus.

When I looked in Roget's Thesaurus I thought it interesting that they noted 13 of the most famous friendships of all time. In this Top 13, one of two from the Bible was the friendship between David and Jonathan.

Friendships are an important part of our lives. Human beings are not made to live in isolation and so throughout our lives we learn how to get on with people, how to talk, relate, help and build each other up. Friends provide great encouragement in the day-to-day activities of our life.

When I left my well paid job in the City and it was clear that I wasn't going back, I was not surprised that many of the friendships I enjoyed, associated with my job, evaporated - I was no longer useful to a lot of people; telephone calls weren't returned, lunches were cancelled and in a very short period of time invitations ceased to arrive. You find out who your real friends are when you make a big change in your life, particularly if it is a change away from what the majority are doing.

Friends are there to encourage each other. However at a deeper level, the friendship is also often based on endorsing each other. If you have a good friend who you always going drinking with and then you decide to stop drinking, the chemistry involved in the friendship will change and it might not survive. If you have both been overweight together and one of you loses the weight and the other doesn't, if you both have husbands and children and one of you gets divorced, such major changes will have a significant impact.

My very best all time friend has got to be Jesus Christ. From the day I committed my life to Christ He has never left my side.
He has been patient with me as I have fumbled along and strayed back into old habits.
He has been faithful and supportive long into the night when I have been lamenting and fretting about all the things He continually tells me not to worry about.
He is creative in coming up with solutions to situations I can't see a way forward on and He waits to complete His sentence when I rush ahead and think I have it figured out by myself. When I come back for the rest of what He was saying He has a twinkle in His eye and continues where He left off.
He smiles at me, hugs me, loves me, nurtures me, encourages me, wipes my tears away, gives me confidence and shows me where other friends of His need my help.
He connects us up.
He sees the whole world and knows all the answers, to all the questions.
He will never ever leave or let me down. He is simply awesome. It's a bit like having your absolutely best friend ever, permanently at the end of a telephone, with no static on the line - you can hear them clearly, you know them so well you can see them and where they are and you know, one day, you will be reunited - how can you be anything but joyful? Your heart just wants to burst with love, love that is fresh and new each day.

One of my favourite Christian songs is by an Australian group, Hillsong, and it is called 'Friends in High Places' :

Well I was in need, I needed a friend
I was alone, I needed a hand
I was going down, but someone rescued me
My God cares too much to say, His mercies are new every day
I get down to pray and then help is on its way.

I walk by faith and not by sight
When things go wrong, I know it'll be alright
'cause someone's watching over me.

I've got friends in high places,
I've got someone I can call
and I've got someone watching over me.

As my faith grows I have begun to recognise that there are two kinds of friends, human ones and spiritual ones. Human friends I connect with in the day-to-day order of my life and spiritual friends I connect with over and above the day-to-day order of my life - a connection within the essence of life. Spiritual friends are those whom I meet in faith and with whom I will spend eternity. Human friends are supported through practical activities; spiritual friends are supported in prayer and by their very nature as a human, we can share all of life's challenges, experiences and joys in both a practical and spiritual dimension.

A very dear friend of mine, who is not a Christian, saw me talking to another one of my friends who is a Christian and said afterwards, "That's the kind of relationship I want with people." I explained to her it's quite straightforward. When you commit your life to Christ the true beauty of the world is revealed to you sometimes step by step and sometimes in a huge wave of revelation. As you grow in that process, you share with others who are travelling on the same journey, perhaps at different stages. Your intimacy and excitement is based on the mutual understanding and acceptance that you are all travelling, willingly, towards the same ultimate goal.

THREE THINGS I HAVE LEARNT

- True friendships evolve naturally and last through tough times.
- You can't solve your friends' problems. You can unconditionally listen to them and be there for them and provide the Kleenex and hugs and spare room if needed.
- Jesus Christ is the best friend you can ever have. He is always with you, always kind, 100% reliable, wise, outstanding sense of humour, very creative, inspiring, motivating and He loves you completely, unconditionally, for who you are.

My Mother never told me:

Pearl of Truth 7:

If you want a friend, be a friend.

CHAPTER EIGHT

Father Christmas is your Dad

The image of Father Christmas is one of a jolly elderly chap, all-knowing about our hearts' desires, someone with a huge bag of goodies to dispense to all those who have behaved themselves well. The first year that I got a Christmas present that I didn't like, want or need, I was disappointed and seriously began to wonder at the truth of Father Christmas. If he was so brilliant at his job, why didn't he know my taste better! It was not that I wanted lots of things, I just wanted the few presents I had to be really right for me, not presents that could suit anyone, but ones that I wanted deep inside, which only someone like Father Christmas could really know about.

My father once gave me an Elvis Presley album. He had asked me what I had wanted and I told him exactly which Elvis album. I was so excited and sure that he would get me what I wanted; instead he got me a different album and it was an 'MFP' (Music for Pleasure) which meant it wasn't even Elvis really singing, but someone who sounded like him. I thanked him hugely, for my father didn't often get me presents, and felt very ungrateful in my heart.

To me, Father Christmas could never have been the Dad I knew, for he didn't live with us, rarely saw us and didn't know what I liked. Therefore to me, someone else has always been involved, someone working behind the scenes, who ensured each year, despite any financial hardships we were facing, there was always a present under a tree, food on the table and a sense of warm family unity. The whole sense of Christmas is wrapped up for me in being at home with people you love; presents are a bonus.

My sister often buys me a present to wear, which I don't even realise I like, want or need. She is used to me opening it and thanking her and then I put it in a cupboard for a long period of time. Surprisingly, at some point, it usually comes out and three or four years after her giving it to me, it will become a firm favourite in my wardrobe - somehow, sometimes, she seems to know my future taste better than I do. I can't explain why I don't take to it straight away. I don't dislike it enough to give it back or have it changed, I just feel the need to put it away and take it out at some later date - very strange and frustrating for her I am sure. The compliment to her is the depth of knowledge she has of me and the care she gives to selecting something personal for me.

Presents are very emotive. At Christmas in particular people wrap them up in beautiful paper and bows, and expectation escalates. As they sit under the Christmas tree, or you are given one and you hold it waiting to open it, you can imagine all sorts of things that can be inside. Your heart may flutter wondering if it is just what you wanted or more than that, almost dared to hope for. If you are somewhat of a calmer person you immediately think, "I know what this is" and dutifully open it in a very straightforward manner, not expecting any surprises in life.

Yet miracles do happen and life can be very surprising, often at the most unexpected times.

As the summer ended I felt strongly that I should take my daughters and go and visit the Rocky Mountains in Canada. This was a challenging thought as I had no money to make the trip and when I looked at all the activities ahead until Christmas the only time we could possibly go, was in the half-term holidays in October. I mused on the thought for a while and dismissed it several times.

Unexpectedly two things happened. Surfing the internet I found extremely inexpensive flights, and exactly the right amount of money to pay for them appeared in my bank account. It seemed providential and I booked the flights.

Although I am Canadian I have not spent much time as an adult in Canada and while my daughters were excited about the forthcoming trip, frankly I didn't really want to go. I had so much to do with work and practical activities at home, I was just as happy staying put. However, the tickets were bought and a commitment had been made so in due course, we packed up our bags and headed for London.

The night before our flight we stayed in Notting Hill Gate and planned to take the A2 bus straight to Heathrow. After a lifetime of international travel I was very laid back about the arrangements and confident of the time we had available to catch the 3:15pm flight. Rather than pottering around waiting to go, at 11am myself and the children decided to catch the next bus and took our luggage down to wait for it.

A black cab taxi driver came by and offered us a lift to the airport for the price of the bus, assuring us he was going that way and it would provide a bit of extra money for his lunch. We hopped in. As we sped away and I couldn't see a disc saying his taxi number and name, I started to get concerned that I had been really foolish jumping in with the two girls. I know London very well and the route he started to take deviated from the way I would have gone and my anxiety level increased significantly. By this time I was praying hard. "Dear Lord, I don't really want to go to Canada, so if we are not meant to go please stop us getting there on time, but Lord keep us safe."

We arrived promptly at Terminal 3 and the driver was courteous and efficient and I felt mean-hearted that I thought he would be anything but sincere. We pushed our luggage into the terminal looking for the check-in desk. The flight was not listed on the screens anywhere. I then thought it must have been cancelled as the tickets were so cheap, however decided rather than jumping to conclusions, the best thing to do was to ask Air Canada for guidance. It was now 11:55am and as we approached an Air Canada official, a new thought was emerging in my mind.

Sure enough, I had got the time wrong. The flight we were booked on was leaving at 1.05pm and the check-in desk was just closing. Air Canada were amazing and rushed us through with our bags; we all ran from the terminal, through security to the gate and onto the plane. As it took off, my older daughter and I looked at each other and said, "We were definitely meant to be going to Canada then!". Had the taxi driver not given us a lift, there is no way we would have made the flight.

A couple of days later as I stood at the foot of the Rockies, with the sun shining and a gentle snow fall all around, as I looked at the majesty of the mountains, my heart was bursting with joy, like someone had given me the best gift ever, the experience of being there, of standing in the country of my birth and feeling a sense of coming home - it was so very beautiful. Despite living by the sea and walking on the beach every day, I realised I had forgotten just how awe inspiring nature was, how surprising it can be. I was really thankful for the opportunity of rediscovering Canada.

It seems to me human nature is often pretty ungrateful. I recall as a child being chastised by my mother if my 'thank you' cards for Christmas and my birthday were not sent out promptly within a week of the event. I can see there is a real selfishness connected with not thanking people, an arrogance that you completely deserved what was given. In actual fact, thanking someone for a gift recognises the relationship involved in the giving and receiving.

Some people are very good at giving yet find it hard to receive. They will generously thrust presents upon you and get very annoyed if you start giving presents back. They may tell you that you can't afford to give them presents and criticise the manner in which you have spent your money (making you feel you wish you hadn't bothered). There is a control element attached to such behaviour and again an arrogance. They do not wish to be beholden to you; by giving and being unwilling to receive, they can keep you at a comfortable distance emotionally.

When the Israelites were liberated from slavery and left Egypt, they soon started moaning about lack of decent grub to eat. Many felt they were better off as slaves as at least they knew where their next meal was coming from. Moses and his brother Aaron had a chat to God about the fact that there were no local supermarkets in the desert and they really needed some kind of miracle to feed a very large group of unhappy, hungry people. As usual, God was way ahead and let them know that bread would be delivered each morning, and meat each evening. The people were told to gather up what they needed for each day for six days and on the sixth day to collect enough for two days, in order that they didn't work on a Sunday.

Imagine what they must have thought when they woke up in the morning of the first day, still really hungry, to find that all around on the ground was an abundance of food, delicious fulfilling food and as much as they could possibly want. In the evening, the same thing happened with quails who flew in and covered the camp. What a miracle from above!

Despite being told not to hoard, some people did, worried that God might not keep it up. When they went into their hoard however they found it was full of worms and smelt rotten and they then had to destroy it before it could contaminate anything.

To me this is historical evidence of how all blessings ultimately come from our Father in heaven, our spiritual Father. As with the food to the Israelites, God might use different methods and people to meet our needs. He will, however, always provide for us abundantly. We in turn need to ensure that we are not hoarding more than we need, that as we are given so we must also give, and give lavishly.

It is inspiring when the popstar sells one of his houses and gives the three million pounds from the sale to a charity; when companies match the amount their employees give to charity - pound for pound; when a friend with two cars gives one to someone in desperate need yet without the ability to buy one; when a Church spontaneously gives the whole of its weekly offering to a woman's refuge in need; when a landlord agrees to his tenants staying on in a property rent-free when they hit hard times and became penniless; in all these situations, people are acting graciously.
Grace is our spiritual Father's greatest gift to mankind.
Robert Farrar Capon said:

"Grace is the celebration of life, relentless hounding of all the non-celebrants in the world. It is a floating, cosmic bash shouting its way through the streets of the universe, flinging the sweetness of its cessations to every window, pounding at every door in a hilarity beyond all liking and happening, until the prodigals come out at last and dance, and the elder brothers finally take their fingers out of their ears."

We seem to live in a world that wants to quantify, justify, analyse and deliberate every move instead of waking up to the liberating reality of living graciously, with love for those around us.

In the 1970's when there was a scare that coffee, and at one point toilet rolls, might be rationed (yes, it's true) I remember going to a friend's house and their pantry was full of coffee and toilet rolls. I understood the toilet rolls better; however, I asked her why, when her parents didn't even drink coffee. Their family was so worried about not having enough for themselves, they hoarded things they didn't even need, causing others who perhaps needed it more to go without. Overall this hoarding tendency was what started to fuel a potentially genuine national shortage. Perhaps if we in the West hoarded less, those countries in desperate need would have more.

God blesses us hugely. As a world, there is a great imbalance between those who have and those who have not. I wish I had known earlier in my life just how much God gives to us, so that I could have thanked him more. The best way I have found to say thank you to God is by being kind and generous to others, with no expectation of a 'thank you' or reward in return for favours or gifts.

I admire greatly the annual 'Operation Christmas Child' activity that the charity Samaritan's Purse undertake. People all over the world are asked to fill a shoebox with small Christmas presents for a child somewhere else in the world who has nothing and no concept of someone called Father Christmas. The charity then organise the delivery of millions of shoeboxes to children in need. Being part of Operation Christmas Child gives you the opportunity to be Father Christmas to as many children as you want: one, five, ten or thousands. The need is limitless and each year, continues to grow.

The very best presents in the world to me are experiences and time with people; God my Father knows that and surprises me with gifts of His time, every day. These gifts have a lasting and priceless value. In our time together He reveals new truths about the world, my life, work and purpose for the day. In my intimate time with Him, through prayer, it is like taking off layers of wrapping paper to reveal the true present, shiny jewels of thought each day. In love with Christ, in relationship with Him, it is like the very best sparkling Christmas every day. As your relationship deepens, you grow in understanding that God the Father, our spiritual Father, knows our hearts' desires, even better than we do.

God gives to us throughout our life and in return His dearest wish, the present He most wants from us, is our heart, our willingness to follow Him, to trust Him, to walk and talk with Him, to be in relationship with Him. As He watches us receive so much, He is longing for us to be thankful with a grateful heart and to demonstrate it through the way we live our lives.

THREE THINGS I HAVE LEARNT

- The heart of Christmas is love, from a Father who loved us so completely, He sent His Son to earth to guide us on our way home.
- Gifts of time are priceless.
- Privilege and responsibility go hand in hand.

My Mother never told me:

Pearl of Truth 8:

Faith is a present waiting to be unwrapped. Locked into our heart is the knowledge that the innocent excitement and anticipation of catching a sight of Father Christmas, is the same feeling we will have when we wait for God to come and surprise us .... which He has promised to do.

CHAPTER NINE

Wine into Lumpy Spuds

Rather than the morning cup of tea, or in my case coffee, my favourite drink of the day is definitely a glass of cold white wine around 7:30pm in the evening when my chores are done. Preferably I like to watch the soap opera Coronation Street and just vegetate in front of the television. Not an exciting start to the evening; however, it is a very comfortable habit. Not only do I enjoy this evening ritual, as I speak to many others I find it is quite a common practice. With a glass of wine in one hand, before I know it, I could easily be mistaken for a couch potato.

My challenge comes when the glass is empty and I contemplate having another and then watching the next programme, or getting on with doing something more constructive. Quite often I have opted for staying put and continuing to indulge myself, arguing that I deserve to relax after such a hectic day. Mondays are the hardest day as there is a continual run of soap opera choices on television, yet it is only the beginning of the week and so if I start drinking wine then, I will struggle through the rest of the week, until Friday which is the best night for enjoying a few glasses of wine.

It takes a considerable amount of self-discipline to restrict myself either to drinking wine only on Friday and Saturday nights, or to limiting myself to one glass on other nights. The knowledge that I have to drive each morning is a really helpful responsibility and I remind myself if something happened in the night and I had to rush out - I wouldn't be able to drive. This is an appropriate reminder, tucked alongside my mother's advice to always wear clean knickers in case you have an accident and have to be attended to by medics.

People have commented that it is 'wrong to drink alone'. I think such a remark comes from Victorian attitudes; after all, millions of people smoke alone each day and there is a stark similarity in the habits. Both habits are comforting and self-indulgent. I rarely go out in the evening as it is expensive to secure babysitters and I dislike smoky places, so enjoying wine at home is one of the ways I unwind.

The other way I have found to unwind is in creating things. I find that making something brings out all sorts of positive feelings in me. One of the materials I like to use is fabric. Many years ago when I returned to Canada to live for a while, I learnt to quilt as one of the ways to keep busy during the long, very cold, Canadian winter. I am not particularly good at quilting however I do love doing it and it has proved to be a useful and practical hobby. In addition, it has the added benefit of being a single-minded activity. I have found it impossible to drink and sew at the same time.

As part of my long term self improvement project and New Year intentions, I decided a couple of years ago to have a whole year of trying not to drink any alcohol. I thought the best way to keep myself busy in this process was to make a huge king size quilt representing the year and all that happened as it unfolded. This was to test myself to see how well I could master my habits. I naturally gave myself a get-out-clause and took the executive decision that if I did decide to have an alcoholic drink (at this point I had started to think ahead to forthcoming events in the year) I would sew in a black square to represent each or any day I may have had some alcohol.

After considerable thought, it made perfect sense to me to stop drinking after New Year's Eve as I had a friend over and we had already planned a good night out in my local, very rowdy pub. Several drinks later, we left the others and headed back to mine for the champagne I had been saving for midnight. Having been single for many years it was quite a surprise to me to find out on New Year's Eve that my friend really fancied me and more, wanted a jolly good New Year's Eve kiss. While it was all wonderful and exciting, in the background my mind was trying to decide whether this constituted one or two black squares.

Over the next few weeks several black squares had to be added. In fact the original size of the square was reduced in order that the quilt didn't look too sombre. Eventually, I won't trouble you with the full story, after a frenzy of activity, a showering of presents and many promises, a wedding date was set, a Church booked, dresses bought and the bridegroom - well, having set the scene, he absconded. Tragically the quilt lies half-unfinished in the bottom of my sewing box. I recognised that had I stuck to my original plan, my year would very likely have evolved differently and the pain of the fall-out would have been significantly reduced.

Alcohol has a lot to answer for. As you can see, I enjoy it! However I also know it can go one of two ways, either lulling you into a level of inactivity which is counter-productive or encouraging you into activity which is destructive. There's a proverb which says:

Who has woe? Who has sorrow?
Who has strife? Who has complaining?
Who has wounds without cause? Who has redness of eyes?
Those who linger late over wine, those who keep trying
mixed wines.

Do not look at wine when it is red, when it sparkles in
the cup and goes down smoothly.
at the last it bites
like a serpent
and stings like an adder.
your eyes will see strange things
and your mind utter perverse things.
and when you awake, you will seek another drink.

This proverb reminds me of several late nights with friends, putting the world to rights over wine. There is a chap in the Bible called Hosea who reckoned that wine took away understanding and made people do daft things. He was an interesting chap. Hosea married a prostitute and gave her a wonderful home where they had three children together. Hosea loved his wife. Unfortunately her old habits were hard to break and she wandered back into her previous life, enjoying the drinking binges and sexual activity with other men. Hosea remained steadfast in his love for her and went down to the place she had returned to and pleaded with her to come home, assuring her of his devoted love.

Friends and family thought he was mad. How could he love someone who had in social terms wronged him so badly. Yet Hosea's whole life was about true and pure love. He believed fully in God and knew that as God willingly forgave him for his wrongdoings and assured him of eternal life, who was he to judge his errant wife? As he recognised the unconditional love which God showered upon him, so he wanted to express this same unconditional love to his wife, his closest companion, mother of his children. Hosea managed to bring her home again.

Hosea was not particularly a religious man, for religion is not the same as faith and not the same as love. Religion is in fact often the easy option used as a bandage to an uneasy conscience or a 'hedging the bets' payment towards the future. Yet God is all knowing and looks further into our actions to really determine the level of love and service demonstrated. It wouldn't have been the same if Hosea had marched into his wife's brothel and demanded she came home. He had to go and beg her to come home with him as he loved her and needed her. For some people, they would judge that Hosea had gone 'too far'. He should have just left her to her own fate.

Yet Hosea recognised that you can never go too far for someone you love, you can never give too much. For me, this was a wonderful revelation and made me feel much more positive about the depth I can feel for people - I would do anything I possibly could for someone I loved and often in my life I have been told 'it is too much' and I have felt guilty. Did I love them too much? Did I give them too much? Did I ask for too much? Here in the security and warmth of the Bible my ancestors, connected to me throughout the generations when I became a Christian, assure me that it is absolutely okay to give all the love you feel inside; as it is given out, it is refilled by God daily.

I once went out with someone whom I loved a great deal. It took me a while to figure out the way he approached things. He explained to me that he kept in his mind a scorechart of who he did what for, and when, and on the other side kept a close account of who did what for him, and when. It was very stressful and complicated to be part of. I loved him for the person I could see he could be, if he would let go and just be the best he could be. In a way I guess I loved the little boy trapped inside the man. I loved him for the days when we walked miles, talked and dreamed lots and had terrific fun. I loved him for his ability to fix technical things which were completely beyond me. Unfortunately control of his environment when other people were involved was a huge factor in his life; he was uncomfortable operating in any other mode. Such a restriction meant that in relationship with him, you could only develop at a par, or below his level, otherwise he would feel very uncomfortable that you were growing ahead of him and that subsequently he might get left behind. I came to release his insecure behaviour was strongly linked to a fear of being abandoned.

Hosea's wife might have behaved very poorly; however, he didn't judge her in any conventional sense. He went after her and questioned whether she would be really happy, in the long term, in the hedonistic life she had chosen, or at home, secure, loved and cared for, watching her children grow up. He didn't force her, he presented the case and she came home.

Through the ages wine has also been used to celebrate events, to have in moderation as a refreshment, to enjoy alone or with others. The caution on the bottle however should be that it can slowly rob you of the days of your life. The analogy that springs to mind is that of the frog:

Put a frog in boiling water and it will jump out
Put a frog in normal water on the stove and a low heat
and as it is comfortably warmed up
it will stay where it is
until eventually it is boiled to death.

What the poor frog needed was someone more experienced in such matters to come along and shout at him that he was not warming himself comfortably; sipping on the water that was freely available, he was dying a slow death, he was drowning - get out while he still

could! Get out while he could still demonstrate energy and an active life! Get out while he could still be effective!
Get out and warn others.

Unfortunately Alcohol distorts your hearing; when you have had a few glasses you can imagine that you are hearing all sorts of things. If you are enjoying yourself it would likely be along the lines of 'I love you'. If you are not happy to start with, it will depress you further and you will start imagining people are saying negative things about you (which leads to many late night fights). I remember going to an opening party at a company I worked for in my teenage years, and the younger ones amongst us being really excited about the prospect of a free bar. After two or three drinks I saw the Managing Director standing to one side with an orange juice and I looked out from his perspective to those partying and saw a very different scene. What to me had seemed so innocent really held many dangers.

White wine my dear can be lethal
Take 2 at the very most
Take 3 and you're under the table
Take 4 and you're under the host!

Those who use drinking as an anaesthetic for pain, to escape from their life however momentarily, inevitably feel worse when they wake up in the morning and the pain is still with them, perhaps increased by their behaviour the night before. Alcohol is a drug, albeit more subtle and socially acceptable than most.

A very beautiful friend of mine was not a regular drinker. Once she was out for the evening however, she would 'get the taste for it'. It might start slowly; however, it would build into mixing spirits, beer and wine.

She was very entertaining when she was drunk and a great encouragement to others.
I stayed over and babysat for her children one night, while her husband was working away, and by 3am I was worried as to what had happened to her. She finally came home at 4am extremely drunk yet seemed very happy.
I helped her to bed and went to bed myself, exhausted.
In the morning I heard her baby crying out continually and thought I should go and check on him.
On the way I looked into her room to see if she was awake. She was lying in bed, covered in vomit, and I thought she was dead.
A thousand thoughts went through my mind and I realised I would not know how to contact her husband if she was. Should I telephone for an ambulance? I raced over to her and moved her slightly when she moaned and I realised thankfully that she was going to be okay.
She opened her eyes and I could see she was still drunk, but encouraged her to get into the shower before the children came in.
At that moment, she didn't look beautiful; she looked a complete and utter mess, vulnerable, wounded and desperate.
An hour later, over a coffee, she very shakily told me of what a great evening she had had, although she felt very guilty about kissing someone she had met in the pub.
A week later, still suffering from mild shakes, she told me of her visit to her doctor who had told her that she had to stop drinking or it would kill her.

When Hosea reached out to his wife, he reached through the haze she was living in and offered her a real, drug free life where she could regain her balance and get things in perspective.

God calls us not to sit on the sidelines and be a spectator to life, but to get active, to get involved, to find out more about others and discover, in that process, more about ourselves.

Rather than numbing our senses, we need to break through the pain barrier we are facing and find freedom to live our lives well.

Once we are dead, it is too late to change.

THREE THINGS I HAVE LEARNT

- The less I vegetate the better I feel.
- Drink a glass of water for every glass of wine you drink; it slows you down and limits headaches.
- If you are using alcohol as a bandage over pain, it makes financial and emotional sense to stop drinking and figure out the pain - on the other side of that process, you will begin to sparkle naturally.

My Mother never told me:

Pearl of Truth 9:

Binge drinking is escapism and it can kill you.

CHAPTER TEN

The Good Life

At work I have always had an analytical approach. In any given situation, I can look at various perspectives and create a workable structure to suit the challenge at hand. In the early 1990's I was very involved with assisting to create structure around mass redundancy programmes. It was a time when thousands of jobs were under threat. Large blue chip organisations were facing the fact that computer systems were coming of age and replacing people. There was a growing need to reorganise the mixture and suitability of people employed in a business with the objectives of the company. Companies which had traditionally found themselves dealing with people face to face, were now exploring the logistics of large call-centres and discussing whether these would be based in the UK or abroad. While these major business decisions were taking place, there was a very human impact brewing which needed careful management.

In one scenario, one of the largest conglomerates in the world needed to reduce their European workforce by several thousand whilst keeping their most talented people happy and motivated. One of my roles was to design a process that would maintain morale and attract positive publicity, while making people redundant and attracting new people, with much needed skills, to the company. It was just the sort of business rubix cube I thrive on. Success was attributable to my constant awareness of, and compassion for, the individuals whose lives were caught up in the major changes taking place.

It was not uncommon for companies to 'dispose' of people on a Friday, after many years of loyal service, only to be ringing them within a couple of weeks requesting that they come back for a short period, as their knowledge was critical to a business function. Short-sighted companies, in the midst of a crisis, seemed to completely overlook the emotional contract that is made between a loyal employee and their employer.

When an employee joins a company, it can be compared to a partnership contract. The employee agrees to become an Ambassador to the company and to utilise all their skills abilities and talents for the benefit of the company. The employee also agrees to be bound by the rules of the company, usually found in a Staff Handbook. The company, in turn, agrees to look after the employee in financial terms although there are usually several other areas which agreements are made on: location of work, team and the hours of commitment it involves. Naturally in any company there are a lot of contracts running at any one time and the 'glue' which holds it all together is framework of agreements around job descriptions, salaries, environment, business ethics and activities.

If you join a business which makes greeting cards and without consultation with you, they change their minds and start making nuclear submarines and want you to move immediately 300 miles away to a labatory on the ocean floor, you would rightly feel that the employer had not been straightforward with you. Should an employer find that their employee had been stealing post-it-notes and selling them on a market stall at the weekends, they would also feel the contract under which the employee was employed, was broken.

In situations where a company is in trouble and has to reduce salaries, but require the staff to maintain hours, the company will need to rely on the quality of the emotional contract with staff if it is to survive. When an employee has a relative who dies and she requires time off to attend to the funeral, she will greatly appreciate the sensitive manner in which the company supports her.

One of the early books I wrote was called 'Corporate Kisses' and it told the true story of how several companies, facing trouble, will start to behave badly, start to step over others in order to get to where they think the future glory lies, start to rewrite employee contracts and to reverse decisions made and commitments given. With no crisis management in place for a new, difficult situation, they can resort to bully boy tactics feeling that the end they might achieve would justify the method of reaching it.

The fact is that circumstances associated with work, change. Companies evolve and their employees either evolve with them, or move into another organisation.

My own feeling is that there should be no difference in the way a company behaves, to that in which an individual behaves. All of us, individually and corporately, need to live with integrity and with a view on our future.

Diversity is a buzz word used frequently in the last few years. In my experience no matter how many focus groups are set up to discuss and perhaps address the challenges facing organisations, the only real change which will have a lasting impact is the change which takes place at the heart of corporate behaviour and therefore the heart of individual behaviour.

There are people who view the Christian faith as quite a negative relationship to be in, one where God has all the power and says no continually to people who say they believe in Him and yet don't seem to be very different to anyone else; they still seem to struggle in life and never look very happy - not an attractive proposition. The truth is that there are a lot of people who call themselves Christian, yet never fully commit to their relationship with God, preferring to maintain an arrangement which is more comfortably tailored to the rest of their life, and one which is less demanding.

God set out ten guidelines for people to follow who want to be in His family and these are (taken from the Street Bible):

1. I am your God, I have liberated you and I get total priority. You must not give your time, attention, love, money or anything else to another god.

2. You are not to idolise anything else. Do not waste time, money or resources on buying, polishing, nurturing or generally loving anything, or anybody else but me because I get jealous - I am your only God. When I am jealous, I get ruthless and punish families even three or four generations after those who hated me have rotted in their graves. If you live by my rules I will show you incredible love and to generations that follow you.

3. Don't use my name lightly as some sort of magic word, supposed to blackmail me into action. Do not use my name as a swear word - if you do, you won't go unpunished. Handle my name with care!

4. You will keep my Rest Day different, distinct, special. You'll do what the word means - "stop". You can work six days, do all you've got to do, then the seventh day is my day. You won't work,

you family won't work, your staff won't work, your equipment won't work, your guests won't work. I made everything in six days, then I took a rest on the seventh. So will you.

5. Treat your parents with respect, then you'll live long and prosper in this new land I am moving you into.

6. Don't snuff out life, stop someone's clock, blow anyone away, bump anyone off, dole out the big chill, erase, drop, hit, top or waste anyone.

7. Don't sleep with someone else's wife or husband, put it about or cheapen yourself.

8. You wont thieve, nick, lift, blag, fleece, half-inch, wipe or get sticky-fingered.

9. You wont lie, fib, fudge about someone, in or out of the witness box.

10. You wont drool over your mate's wife or husband, house, garden, staff, equipment, gadgets or anything else they have and you don't.

and later, a further directive was added:

11. Love one another, even at the cost of personal suffering.

If you enter into a Covenant (emotional contract) with God, and keep to His guidelines, He will honour His side of the contract to you and provide for you abundantly all the days of your life and on into eternity. His guidelines never change. He never renegotiates the basic agreement. He never has and never will. He is completely reliable.

God's timeframe however isn't ours and as you follow Him, you learn that faith and trust go hand in hand.

After my being unemployed in Cornwall for almost a year, the debtors were pressing in and the overdraft had escalated. I needed to sell our home, to realise capital from it to repay debts I had accumulated. It was a very emotional decision to take; however, the house we were then going to move to, although smaller, was in a great community. We exchanged and completed in one day, the removal men came and we were left with our clothes and no roof over our heads. A friend stepped in and we went to live with them while the new purchase was completed. The next day the sellers of the house we were to move to, pulled out of the sale. We were homeless.

At testing times it is interesting to see whether we consider the glass is 'half empty' or 'half full'.

The next five months proved to be an intense period of inactivity, desperation, resolution, exercise and diet and spiritual reflection.
Up until that point, I had been a Christian, although quite a Sunday Christian (I went to Church on Sunday and tried to be good). However in that period, it felt like I was living in a wilderness, that I had been forgotten by God, abandoned with my children. It was really hard to take. What had I done that was so bad this dreadful circumstance should have befallen us? I felt angry and frustrated all at the same time. When I had finished moaning about my situation I started to look around for some answers to help us move forward. I started to really enjoy the fact that I wasn't driving myself so hard and I started to enjoy time with people in a way I hadn't for years. For the first time, perhaps ever, I was learning to relax.
The friend I had gone to live with was in the midst of a very difficult

financial time and it helped that I had some cash in the bank; we were able to support each other in different ways. We went on several diets together to make the most of being poor and laughed more than I had done in years. We walked miles together as we had no money for petrol, and with the children made plans to travel to various foreign countries. We spent our days applying for jobs and most evenings we gazed out over the ocean and contemplated how challenging life was.

In time myself and my children were rescued by a wealthy relative and we moved into a house in the same village as my friend. In all of this I could see how God was moving in our lives; my faith was deepening and my reliance on Him growing. When my relative bought a house for us to live in, I was overjoyed at how God had moved to repair family relationships which were strained. Although the relative did not profess to believe in God, I could see the grace with which they had helped us and it had God's hallmark on it. As the pace of my life slowed down considerably, I started to discover so many more positive aspects of my character; I started to realise I could be of help to people in new ways. Enabled by daily prayer and bible study, I chilled out more, mellowed, continue to laugh more than I had ever done before and found a real release in living an honest, simple life, in service to others.

One of my all time favourite British comedies is 'The Good Life', situated in Surbiton on the fringes of London. Tom and Barbara opt out of City Life and decide to start living in a self sufficient manner. They decide to turn their backs on the politics of working in a large company. Their neighbours and best friends next door, the Ledbetters, think they are both mad; however they stand beside them as friends, as they change their world around. In the final programme of the series, while Tom and Barbara are next door their home is broken into and vandals, not finding anything worth taking, trash the house. On their return it seems that they will have to give up the way of life they have created, for the calamity which has befallen them is too great to bear. However, unbidden from the depth of their heart they start to talk about the animals in the garden and the day to day problems, apart from the vandalised room, which need addressing. Slowly they build themselves up, dust themselves off and continue on their journey. The four friends stand together and toast 'The Good Life'.

There are times in life when circumstances threaten to overtake us. I don't know how people cope without faith, for who do you turn to when you are all alone? A dear friend of mine is an avid yoga student and I struggled to see the attraction. She feels no need of Christianity as she has found her calm and well being in her yoga. I listened as she talked at length of the movements which she enjoyed most in the exercise and as she talked I could see similarities between what keeps her going as a yoga student and what keeps me going as a Christian. The real difference became clear when she described the 'prayer position' and I realised that how at the very point she reaches that perfect position, it is similar to when I enter the Lord's presence through heartfelt prayer;
in her position, temporarily and ultimately she is alone,
in mine I meet Jesus Christ and He takes my load and refreshes me eternally.
In hers, the experience is limited to her own contentment.
In Christ, all are welcome, all can share His abundant joy and love.

The emotional contract we feel for those close to us, those at work or those in other lands, is reflected in the way we live our lives.
If you really don't care very much about other people, or feel compassion for their situation you are unlikely to attract people to your

own life with depth of feeling for you.

Firmly anchored in your relationship to Christ, as you reach out to others, you will find a wealth of love poured out to you.

THREE THINGS I HAVE LEARNT

- God sees a sincere heart and encourages us on.
- Exploring the emotional contracts you have in your life gives you a new perspective on how you view things and shows you where positive structure in your life exists, highlighting also where it doesn't.
- Something worth having, is worth working for and worth fighting for.

My Mother never told me:

Pearl of Truth 10:

Being a Christian is a truly Good Life.

THE PARABLE OF THE HIDDEN TREASURE AND THE PEARL

"The kingdom of heaven is like treasure hidden in a field.
When a man found it, he hid it again, and then in his joy
went and sold all he had and bought that field.
Again, the kingdom of heaven is like a merchant
looking for the fine pearls.
When he found one of great value, he went away and
sold everything he had and bought it.

(Matthew 13:44-45)

The New City

The twelve gates were twelve pearls,
Each gate made of a single pearl.
The great street of the city was of pure gold, like transparent glass.
The City does not need the sun or the moon to shine on it,
for the glory of God gives it light.
Nothing impure will ever enter it, nor will anyone
who does what is shameful or deceitful.

(From the Book of Revelation Chapter 21)

I dare you to be different and change the way you live
Just turn your whole world upside down, accept what Jesus gives
Give up the dark, walk in God's light that others cannot see
I dare you be different, I dare you to be free.

I dare you, try being good, its easy to be had
Its hard to do what Jesus says when friends all think you're mad
But with God's help you'll have the strength to win the conscience fight
I dare you be different, and stand for what is right.

I dare you be different in what you say and do
And try to be a friend of God, He's been a friend to you
And when they say you're upside down or that you're round the bend
I dare you, stay right with God, it's worth it in the end.

(Written by Steve & Kay Morgan-Gurr)

Photographs:

With thanks to Nick Bailey for main photographs including cover.
Pearl photographs by Joy Batten.

Charity information:

Did you know that if you pay tax in the UK, for every £1 you give to charity, they can claim a further £0.28 back from the government, sign a Charity Declaration note for each charity you forward money to.

SAMARITAN'S PURSE INTERNATIONAL
Limited, Victoria House, Victoria Road, Buckhurst Hill, Essex IG9 5EX
www.samaritanspurse.org

AMNESTY INTERNATIONAL UK,
99 - 119 Rosebery Avenue, London, EC1R 4RE
www.amnesty.org.uk

UNICEF,
Africa House 64-78 Kingsway WC2B 6NB London United Kingdom
www.unicef.org

OXFAM,
274 Banbury Road, Oxford OX2 7DZ, United Kingdom
www.Oxfam.org.uk

OPEN DOORS,
PO Box 6, Witney, Oxon OX29 6WG, United Kingdom
www.opendoorsuk.org

Acknowledgements

Song: *I Dare you to be Different*: Written by Steve & Kay Morgan-Gurr
2001 Daybreak Music Limited, Silverdale Road, Eastbourne, East Sussex BN20 7AB

I hope you dance: Ronan Keating, 10 Years of Hits published by Universal/MCA Music and written by Tia Sillers and Mark D Sanders.

Introduction: Galations Chapter 5 verse 22

Chapter 1: Serious Concerns by Wendy Cope published by Faber and Faber ISBN 0-571-16705-5
Bible Reference: the Book of Ruth

Chapter 2: I Remember, I Remember from Selections from The Golden Treasury of Poetry, Golden Press New York Copyright 1959, Printed in the USA 1968 Edition.
Bible Reference: the Book of Esther

Chapter 3: Helen Steiner Rice: And the Greatest of These is Love published by Hutchinson ISBN: 0091794129
Bible Reference: Judges Chapter 11 verses 1-33

Chapter 4: Changing Values: How to Find Moral Truth in Modern Times written by David Attwood printed by Paternoster Publishing ISBN: 0-85364-806-9
No Sex Please We're Single written by Ian Stuart Gregory and printed by Kingsway Communications ISBN: 1-84291-038-8
Bible Reference: Genesis 19

Chapter 5 The Purpose Driven Life, written by Rick Warren, published by Zondervan ISBN 0-310-21074-7
Bible Reference: Book of Daniel 4

Chapter 6 Bible Reference: 1 Kings Chapter 10

Chapter 7 Hillsong Music Australia: PO Box 1195 Castle Hill, NSW 1765
Friends in High Places, words and music by Russell Fragar
www.hillsongmusic.com.au
Friendship by Ralph Waldo Emerson printed by Souvenir Press ISBN 0-285-62843-7
How to win friends and influence people written by Dale Carnegie. Printed by Cedar Books an imprint of William Heinemann Limited ISBN: 0-434-11119-8
Bible Reference:
1 Samuel Chapter 9 on through to 2 Samuel Chapter 1

Chapter 8 Love in a Box: Operation Christmas Child ISBN: 1-85078-366-7
www.paternoster-publishing.com
Bible Reference: Exodus 16

Chapter 9 Bible References:
Proverbs 23 29-35 and Hosea Chapter 4. verse 11

Chapter 10 Bible Reference: Exodus 16
Quoted from The Street Bible, printed by Zonervan
ISBN: 0 00 7107900